SECRETS OF

THE MAYA EMPIRE

Camelot
EDITORA

DISCOVER OUR
BOOKS BY READING
THIS QR CODE

President: Paulo Roberto Houch
MTB 0083982/SP

Editorial Coordination: Paola Houch
Art Coordination: Rubens Martim (cover)
Translation: Suellen Durães
Edition: Ana Vasconcelos (ECO Editorial)
Layout: Patrícia Andrioli
Images: Shutterstock

Legal deposit has been made.

International Cataloging-in-Publication (CIP) data according to ISBD	
C181s	Camelot Editora Secrets Of The Maya Empire / Camelot Editora. - Barueri : Camelot Editora, 2024. 144 p. ; 15,1cm x 23cm ISBN: 978-65-6095-047-4 1. Império Maia. 2. Cultura Maia. I. Título.
2023-3754	CDD 972.81016 CDU 7.031.85
Prepared by Odilio Hilario Moreira Junior - CRB-8/9949	

Rights reserved to
IBC — Brazilian Institute of Culture LTDA
CNPJ 04.207.648/0001-94
Avenida Juruá, 762 — Alphaville Industrial CEP.
06455-010 — Barueri/SP
www.editoraonline.com.br

TABLE OF CONTENTS

Statue of Tlaloc located in the museum in Chapultepec, Mexico

INTRODUCTION

Along with the Aztecs and the Inca, the Maya were one of the three largest Amerindian civilizations in Mesoamerica. Great builders – including pyramids – their legacy was extensive not only in architecture, but in medicine, mathematics, astronomy and the arts. They were great traders and the transport of goods, buying and selling of products interconnected their villages, kingdoms and cities, which occupied the current regions of the Yucatan peninsula, Guatemala, Belize, Mexico, Honduras and El Salvador.

In this work, we take you on a dive into the past of this fantastic civilization. You will learn about the origins and people who formed the Maya, the mores, daily life in the cities, science, architecture, commerce, the arts and the polytheistic religion with its human sacrifices. You will also understand why this is the most complex civilization in Mesoamerica, its growth, peak and decline and how, even today, the Maya and their descendants form considerable populations throughout the region and keep a set of traditions and beliefs alive in many countries.

1

ORIGIN AND HISTORY

THE MAYA STILL INSPIRE FEAR AND FASCINATION
AS THEY DID SEVERAL CENTURIES AGO, FOR
THEIR CITIES BURIED IN THE JUNGLE AND FOR
THE MYSTERIES THAT SURROUND THEM

When the Spanish arrived in the regions of Guatemala and the Yucatán peninsula, and came into direct contact with some people who were, in a certain way, descendants of the Maya branches, they had no idea of the size of the civilization they encountered. "It had been six or seven centuries since the classic Maya splendor had been extinguished; and the cities in ruins, devoured by the tropical forest, were mostly forgotten", says researcher Paul Gendrop, in the work *A Civilização Maia*, about the moment of the meeting between the two civilizations.

In fact, the Maya created some of the greatest buildings in Mesoamerica and were, along with the Aztecs and the Incas, one of the three greatest Amerindian civilizations of all time. Their legacy was such that through trade, their villages, kingdoms and cities occupy the current regions of the Yucatán peninsula, Guatemala, Belize, Mexico, Honduras and El Salvador. Knowledgeable in fields such as mathematics, astronomy, not to mention the arts, they were considered the most complex among all Mesoamerican peoples.

THE BEGINNING OF SEDENTARY PEOPLES

There are several theories about the arrival of man on the American continent. The most well-founded theory would be that of passage through the Bering Strait, at a time when ice would have covered much of the territory and the continent would have been linked to Asia. However, this possibility does not rule out the alternative of contacts across the Pacific Ocean or Atlantic Ocean.

"Human activity in the area of Mexico and neighboring Guatemala dates back 20 thousand years or more, to the times when the first hunter-gatherers settled in this area", says Charles Phillips, in the work *The Aztec and Maya World*, about the beginning of Mesoamerican everyday life.

In fact, the retreat of the ice, approximately in the eighth millennium B.C., led to many changes, from the interruption of the passage to Asia, which caused the American continent to be completely isolated from the rest of the world, except for maritime contacts. This isolation, on the other hand, generated greater use by civilizations of their resources, mainly originality, with a primitive subsistence life based on hunting, fishing and collecting native plants and fruits.

THE ANCESTORS AND CONTEMPORARIES OF THE MAYA

The complexity of the people of Mesoamerica can be felt through all the civilizations that were born and extinguished in that region. The history of these peoples has been put to the test since the first nomadic settlements. These nomadic people, in turn, walked across the vast lands of what would later become the Maya Empire. Check out some of the civilizations that were present and others that had already disappeared when the Maya reached the Classic Period of their Empire (between A.D 250 and 900).

THE ZAPOTEC

One of the civilizations that had close cultural ties with the Maya, the Olmec, and the Teotihuacanos was the Zapotec. Also known as "people of the clouds", thanks to the location of their homes, they were one of the key people in the construction of Mesoamerica. Inhabitants of the mountains south of the Mesoamerican highlands, more specifically in the Oaxaca Valley region, outlined the bases of their culture during the Preclassic Period, until the end of the Classic Period, which ranges between 500 B.C and A.D 900. Their capital was founded first on Monte Albán and then on Mitla. The

In Dainzu, there are large stone figures that narrate in a primitive way, in reliefs, some players with helmets and protections, practicing some type of sport, more familiar with the popular ball game, which spread throughout Mesoamerica.

Stone details can also be found in Monte Albán. The city was declared a World Heritage Site by Unesco in 1987

Zapotec dominated that region and made their capitalat a strategic point, overlooking three main valleys, which allowed them to see anyone approaching.

At an altitude of 1,300 feet, the city of Monte Albán has become the economic, religious and residential center for more than 25 thousand people. "An army of workers leveled the uneven ground and built a square paved with white stucco. [...] Monte Albán had become the first city in Mesoamerica", states Charles Phillips in the work *The Aztec and Maya World*.

Despite keeping the capital distant, the Zapotec had agrarian communities in and around the Oaxaca Valley, which facilitated exchanges with other civilizations. At its peak, there were more than a thousand settlements spread throughout the Valley. The mound also became a burial site for Zapotec royalty for several centuries. The population in the golden periods of civilization reached 25 thousand inhabitants, although between A.D 400 and 700 this population remained at an average of 20 thousand.

Despite the communities being focused on agriculture, nothing prevented Zapotec cities from showing a high level of sophistication in their architecture, arts, writing and engineering of various projects. More than 15 palaces built for the Zapotec elite were identified, in addition to those in the capital, around the valleys, which shows that the Zapotec were divided into three distinct groups.

The first was located in the Zapotec Valley, based on the Valley of Oaxaca, the second was in the Sierra Zapoteca, further north, and the third and last was to the south and east in the dependencies of Tehuantepec. The sophistication of the Zapotec was not restricted to their palaces. In Hierve El Agua there is a complex irrigation system that makes it possible to artificially supply constructed terraces, using only natural sources.

This narrative in stone is considered proof of the exchanges and cultural ties between the civilizations that shared the same region. It is known, for example, that in Teotihuacan there was even an entire neighborhood of the city reserved for the Zapotec community, showing the closeness of their relations.

THE ZAPOTEC RELIGION

Just like other peoples present in Mesoamerica, the Zapotec had a very rich pantheon, mainly aligned with the elements of nature.

In those times, civilizations linked natural events to the will and power of deities. Some of the most important gods were the god Bat, responsible for fertility; Beydo, the god of maize, seeds and wind; Cocijo, who in addition to having characteristics of a jaguar and a serpent in a human body, was the god of rain and lightning; and Copijcha, the god of the sun and war, largely symbolized by a macaw. These deities received offerings, prayers, and even human sacrifices seeking favorable intervention in worldly affairs, such as bringing rain, ending droughts, or bringing fertility to the land.

It was also very common, in Mesoamerican cultures, for some days to have glyphs that represented fundamental elements of the population's daily life, since these drastically affected their lives. In the case of the Zapotec civilization, these elements could be like the glyph of Xoo, meaning earthquake, or Pija, meaning drought.

THE DECLINE

The reasons why the cities inhabited by the Zapotec civilization collapsed is still a mystery to archaeologists and experts. There is no trace whatsoever that indicates violent destruction of the sites. The fact also coincides with the fall of Teotihuacan, at a time when conflicts between city-states were frequent, which only supports the theory that these conflicts had some connection with the fall of the Zapotec. In any case, the Zapotec have not completely disappeared. During the Postclassic Period, a smaller center was established in the city of Mitla, called Lyobaa, which in their dialect means "place of rest". The site continued to be occupied even with the Spanish conquests, and to this day it has a sacred significance.

THE OLMEC

The Olmec civilization was one of many that, like its "sisters", played a fundamental role not only in the cultural exchange among these peoples, but also in influencing them. Prosperous in Mesoamerica, they were one of the most powerful people that ever passed through those lands, and established their society between the years 1500 B.C to 400 B.C. In most cases, it is also considered to be the mother civilization of all other Mesoamerican cultures, including the Aztecs and Maya. Located in the Gulf of Mexico, in a territory that today is home to the Mexican states of Veracruz and Tabasco, its domain extended across lands that reached what is now Nicaragua.

Among their contributions to Mesoamerican cultures are ball games, chocolate and animal-like gods. However, it is believed that the Olmec were the first to settle on a plot of land and begin a "sedentary life", abandoning nomadic customs.

THE THREE GREAT OLMEC CENTERS

The Olmec were responsible for the first major centers ever built in Mesoamerica. The most notorious were San Lorenzo, La Venta and Laguna de los Cerros, and each had its own function.

According to Jill Rubalcaba in her work *Empires of the Maya*, with the consultancy of Angela H. Keller, a doctor in archeology and specialist in Mesoamerica, each of the three centers controlled a vital resource for the Olmec and the entire region. "In the east, La Venta dominated the fertile coastal plain where the Olmec grew maize (corn), cacao (the plant from which chocolate is made), and rubber, and extracted salt from ocean waters", states Rubalcaba.

The capital of the empire was San Lorenzo and its peak was between 1200 and 900 B.C. Thanks to its privileged location, in the center of the Olmec territory, it was possible to prevent the capital from suffering from local floods. Among the most valuable goods available to the Olmec for free exchange and trade were obsidian, jade, serpentine, mica, rubber, ceramics, as well as highly polished mirrors, made from magnetite and ilmenite.

Around 900 B.C., the capital was transferred to La Venta, where a population of more than 18 thousand people settled. The reasons behind the ruin of San Lorenzo as a capital are not yet known, but evidence has been found by archaeologists that there was systematic destruction.

All three cities, San Lorenzo, La Venta and Laguna de los Cerros, possessed a type of bilateral symmetry that made them unique. La Venta, for example, was the first city in Mesoamerican history to have a pyramid. The Olmec considered the mountains sacred, however, given their absence in the region, they built the Great Pyramid to perform religious rituals.

THE OLMEC COMMERCIAL CENTERS

Chalcatzingo was one of the largest commercial centers of the Olmec. Located in the Morelos region, it was located in the valley of the Amatzinac River and established three trade routes through which much of the Olmec wealth passed. The wealth of Olmec commerce and especially its commercial centers was such that it was possible to see public areas developing as early as a thousand years B.C, according to Charles Phillips in the work *The Aztec and Maya World*. "Before 1100 B.C, Chalcatzingo had a public area paved with stones and two platforms, also covered with stones, approximately 6 feet high", says Charles in his work.

Between 700 and 500 B.C, Chalcatzingo reached its peak. Maximum prestige appeared with contact with other peoples, such as Monte Albán, capital of the Zapotec, Izapa, on the Pacific coastal plain, and even La Venta, one of the largest Olmec cities.

Pyramids of Chalcatzingo, in the Mexican state of Morelos: important commercial center

Another large Olmec center was Teopantecuanitlán, which was located in the region of Guerreiro. Thanks to constant contact with Chalcatzingo, and through its complex transportation system across the Cuautla, Amacuzac and Balsas rivers, the precious stones trade flourished.

Tin, copper and jade were some of the stones transported to the Pacific Ocean by the Olmec of Teopantecuanitlán. In 600

B.C., for example, they had already become one of the largest centers in that region, further south. "A pyramid and two ball courts were built, and the remains of marine mollusks found in the region could mean that this settlement had links with maritime trade networks", says Charles Phillips in his work *The Aztec and Maya World.*

Near Oaxaca, several villages that began to establish trade with San Lorenzo, the Olmec capital, and among them the one that stood out the most was San Jose Magote. In addition to San Jose Magote having been an important crafts center, where artisans were housed according to their specialties in one of the town's four neighborhoods, the village was responsible for creating part of the Olmec mythology. This is because two Olmec lineages notably grew in that location. One of the families was linked to the figure of a human with the face of a jaguar, which today archaeologists interpret as a representation of the earth. The other family was related to a fiery serpent, which experts believe to be a representation of lightning. In any case, Olmec trade was one of the main reasons for cultural exchange between different Mesoamerican peoples, and was followed, later, by several civilizations, such as the Maya and the Aztecs.

OLMEC ART

In the field of arts, the greatest Olmec legacy - which can be seen to this day - are the wide and majestic stone heads. Made with large basalt stones, in a single facial expression, they are interpreted by historians as portraits of ancient rulers. They can be up to 9.8 feet tall and weigh up to 8 tons. Ten of a total of 17 stone heads were discovered on the premises of San Lorenzo, the ancient Olmec capital.

In most cases, the ruler had his head carved in basalt with a helmet, which represented him as a great warrior, or with a jaguar carved on the back of his neck, which indicated a political and religious symbol of power. Some Mesoamerican cultures had the belief that it was the head that contained the soul, which may provide a possible explanation for the reasons behind the Olmec producing only gigantic heads and not full-body sculptures. In addition to sculpture, pottery and painting were another powerful method of work for the Olmec culture.

THE OLMEC AND THE MAYA

The Olmec were, for some time, contemporaries of the Maya. The influence that the Olmec had on Maya society was very important. In both cultures, it is possible to see the production of monumental thrones, the representation of dead rulers in heads, as well as similar styles in the construction of altars. All of this was done in a similar way in both civilizations. The main detail, however, concerns the representation of a ruler sitting inside an open mouth. In the format of a statue, this figure symbolized, in both cultures, the entrance to the cave that led to the underworld.

Beyond the mythology and the representation of the world of the dead, the architectural projects made for public and ceremonial buildings, the residential constructions of the elite and the houses of the people - it was all influenced by the Olmec. The disappearance of the Olmec, in 400 B.C., coincides with the growth of the Maya civilization and the transition of its historical periods, which indicates that this massive influence between the two cultures happened gradually.

THE LEGACY AND THE ENIGMA

The Olmec legacy can be seen in the most diverse civilizations that progressed in Mesoamerica, particularly in the areas of sculpture, ceramics and the arts, as well as religious systems. The latter was accompanied by the Aztecs and Maya through the incorporation of the god of the Feathered Serpent, who in the Mayan culture was called Kukulcan, and represented one of the greatest gods in the pantheon, while in the Aztec culture this serpent was called Quetzalcoatl. Artistic influences can also be seen in the architecture, the monumental pyramids, the sacrifices and rituals, as well as sports.

THE AZTEC

The Aztec Empire was one of the most notorious ever developed within the entire American continent and, together with the Incas and the Mayans, makes up the triad of the greatest Amerindian civilizations that have ever existed. Founded in 1345, the Aztec Empire reigned over a large expanse of land that covered most of northern and northwestern Mesoamerica, and was responsible for one of the most brilliant and warlike civilizations ever seen. At its peak, the Aztecs had around 60,000 square miles of dominated area and their capital had more than 200,000 inhabitants during the 16th century, which gave it the title of largest city in Mesoamerica. The Aztec population, at its peak, numbered just over 11 million people.

Among the Aztecs' greatest contributions are their temples and pyramids, as well as their irrigation systems, flood-proof dikes, and arts. Barbara A. Somervill, in her work *Empire of the Aztecs*, compares this civilization with other great empires, such as the Roman and Persian. "The Aztecs did not dominate huge areas of land, as did other great ancient empire-builders. (...)The Aztecs united different peoples under their rule. (...) The Aztecs controlled their empire for more than 100 years. Only the invasion of the Spanish, beginning in 1519, ended their rule.", recounts Barbara A. Somervill in her work.

TENOCHTITLAN

The Aztec capital of Tenochtitlan, located on Lake Texcoco, in the region that is now Mexico, was the largest pre-Columbian city in history, and in its heyday, had more than 200,000 inhabitants on its lands. These inhabitants were divided into a caste system that operated throughout the empire. This social stratification was apparently fixed, but historians have already discovered signs of movement between some of them, especially the lowest ones.

The local rulers remained at the top of the castes, called teteuhctin, followed by the local nobles and elite just below the pyramid, called pipiltin, according to the local dialect. Below the local elite were the common citizens, who were called macehualtin, while below them there were only slaves, called tlacohtin. All these citizens were needed to make a capital that was not only political, but religious and very productive as a commercial center.

The trade of goods and raw materials was constant, in addition to ready-made products made from gold, nephrite, turquoise, cocoa, tobacco and cotton, as well as all weapons, tools and ceramic products, which enabled continued progression for the Aztecs and their empire. The creation of canals that transported and managed the water that entered the city was of the utmost importance since the chinampas – elevated fields intended for cultivation – could be harmed.

"The use of chinampas did not die out with the end of the Aztec Empire. They are still used today in a region southeast of Mexico

City, particularly near a lake called Xochimilco. Farmers grow maize, flowers, and vegetables on their island farms", explains Barbara A. Somervill in her work *Empire of the Aztecs*.

RELIGION

Mythology and religion have always been two areas that were very present in the daily lives of ancient people, and this was no different with the Aztecs. The Aztecs were intimately intertwined with the gods and, as proof of this, the name Aztec came directly from Aztlan, the name of the legendary first home of these people. Other Aztec legends suggest that Huitzilopochtli, the patron god of the Aztecs, gave the people an original name, which was Mexica. Even the origin of the place in which they chose to establish their home and capital was made by the gods. The Aztec pantheon was vast and included a mixture of several Mesoamerican gods, that is, common to other civilizations, as well as gods that were exclusively Aztec. The two main Aztec gods were the aforementioned Huitzilopochtli, god of war and the sun, and Tlaloc, the god of rain.

The timing of many of the religious rites, and even agricultural practices, was based on the astronomy studies of the Aztecs, although these were not as accurate as the studies carried out by the Mayans. Thanks to these sacred and religious rites, the gods were honored with parties, banquets, music, dance and small gestures that ranged from the burning of incense and the decoration of statues, to large offerings, such as penances and human and animal sacrifices. "Human beings, adults and less commonly children, were also often sacrificed to metaphorically 'feed' the gods and keep them happy lest they become angry and make life difficult for humans by sending storms, droughts etc., or even just to keep the sun coming out each day", says Barbara A. Somervill in her work.

ARCHITECTURE AND ART

When the Spanish invaded Aztec territory, they were impressed by the splendor and magnificence of the buildings of that people, especially the temples and pyramids made of massive carved stones. This is because the Aztecs represented all subjects through the arts, not just architecture. However, constructions such as the

Templo Mayor pyramid, located in Tenochtitlan, sought to replicate the mount of the great sacred serpent of Aztec mythology.

Aztec art was fine and sumptuous and its artisans could specialize in different types of materials or areas of activity, such as metallurgy, sculpture in stone or wood or even objects that put into practice their skills with crystals, gold, silver and exotic feathers. One of the most interesting details in all of Aztec art is that, in addition to being producers, they were collectors. As great appreciators of the human artistic movement, they brought varied art articles from all parts of the empire to be brought together in Tenochtitlan. These pieces, in turn, were used in Aztec ceremonies and that is why many were buried. However, Aztec art was eclectic and could range from massive pieces such as large pyramids or large murals, to small miniatures set in precious stones.

TEOTIHUACAN, THE SPLENDID CITY

Teotihuacán is one of the most splendid and fascinating cities ever discovered in Central America and, currently, it is the place that receives the most visitors of all the archaeological sites of Mesoamerican peoples.

Located in the northwest zone of the Valley of Mexico, the city was home to around 200 thousand inhabitants in its heyday, having been one of the pillars - and an incomparable cultural nucleus - within societies considered "classic", as shown by Charles Phillips with the consultancy of David M. Jones, doctor in American archeology from the University of London, in the work *The Aztec and Maya World*. "The city reached its maximum splendor in 500 B.C, with 125 thousand to 200 thousand inhabitants, which made it the sixth most populous city in the world at that time", state Charles Phillips and David M. Jones in the work *The Aztec and Maya World*.

The Teotihuacanos, as they were later called by scholars, saw their civilization flourish from 150 B.C. until A.D. 600, when their fall occurred. By the year A.D. 150, the city had already covered an area of approximately 12 miles.

Contemporary with the classic Maya period, it received influence from various peoples, such as the Maya, Aztec and Zapotec civilizations. However, its greatest influence was the Olmec, a people whose society was formed before Teotihuacan.

This influence among all civilizations was such that Teotihuacan is the name given by the Aztecs to the city, since the original name, given by the people who lived in this great center, has not yet been deciphered from the griffins that have stood the test of time.

There are some theories about the origins of the people who lived in Teotihuacán, however, the most likely is that a large part of the people came from other places in the Mexico Basin. This migration, in turn, led to the encounter of cultures and the formation of a large city-state, as demonstrated by researcher and professor at Arizona State University, George L. Cowgill, in the work *The Social Construction of Ancient Cities*. "The early period of rapid growth of Teotihuacan seems to have been accompanied by the near depopulation of the rest of the Basin of Mexico. About 80 to 90 percent of the population was, for a time, concentrated in the city", claims researcher George L. Cowgill. In fact, this is one of the factors, in addition to the city's rich trade and administrative system, that made the Teotihuacanos prosper.

TRADE AND DEVELOPMENT

Much of Teotihuacan's success came from the prosperity of its commerce, which had a neighborhood only for merchants and workers. One of the major raw materials used by the Teotihuacanos was obsidian, taken directly from the Pachuca region, near the city. Obsidian was one of the most valuable stones in Mesoamerica, precisely because of its uses. In the case of Teotihuacan, spears were manufactured, as well as other types of weapons that were later traded with other people.

"Many artisans and merchants lived and worked in the city. The influence of Teotihuacan was so notorious and far-reaching that it could almost be called an Empire. It expanded through trade and exchange and not through war or the threat of military force", states Charles Phillips in his work *The Aztec and Maya World*. Even the Maya city of Kaminaljuyú, located in the Guatemala Valley, came under the influence of Teotihuacan, due to the obsidian trade. "Perhaps marriages between the elites of the two cities occurred. Teotihuacán traders also founded a center in Matacapán, Veracruz, in A.D 400 - 500", adds Charles Phillips in his work.

Other products that could be traded around the city were cotton, salt, cocoa to make chocolate, exotic feathers and shells. In general, much of their food could also be sold, such as maize, beans, pumpkin, tomatoes, avocados, cactus and peppers. The existence of these foods also proves that the Teotihuacanos had a well-balanced diet, which combined all these vegetables, fruits and grains with hunting animals such as deer, rabbits and wild pigs.

TEOTIHUACAN ART

Art is another great element that can be found in the civilization of Teotihuacan, which represented its stories and mythologies through sculpture, ceramics and murals made in the highest and most minimalist style. The art of Mesoamerican civilizations played a unique role in the work of archaeologists and historians, since the artistic styles of each civilization could be found in the territories of other peoples, demonstrating a very large cultural exchange. "Among the inhabitants of Teotihuacán were skilled potters, makers of disturbing masks and extraordinary architects of monuments. However, mural painting was, without a doubt, the art in which they stood out the most", states Charles Phillips in the work *The Aztec and Maya World*.

These murals were created from A.D 300 onwards, as decorative art for the city's main avenue, Avenue of the Dead. After the creations on the avenue, the Teotihuacanos dedicated themselves to sculpting and painting their murals on the Pyramids of the Sun and Moon.

Many of these murals contain deities in their images. Some of these deities are specific to the Teotihuacan civilization, while others are represented in other cultures, such as the god of the Feathered Serpent, whom the Aztecs called Quetzalcóatl.

THE TECHNIQUE OF MURAL PAINTINGS

These murals, in turn, took a very long time to produce, and took days of work from painters whose greatest characteristic was patience. This is because the technique used to produce these murals was archaic and required waiting for a layer of paint to dry so that another could be applied over the previous one. As a first step, artists prepared the walls and walls of temples, pyramids or even the Avenue of the Dead, applying a layer of clay to them, which was later covered by a layer of lime mixed with quartz and sand. Once this step had been completed, the wall was ready to receive its first layers of paint, always reddish in color. Red was always the color chosen because it was a fill color, as if the Teotihuacanos chose it as a "background". After the red was applied, the drawings were worked on in colors such as black and dark blue, which had the function of outlining the lines of the figures in the work. After this stage, it was only necessary to incorporate the colors that would bring the work to life, such as green, yellow and light blue.

SCULPTURE AND MASKS

Among the other works made by Teotihuacan artists, it is worth highlighting the clay objects, the statuettes and the stone masks. The latter was carved using jade, basalt, green stone and andesite. The choice of ores for the production of masks guaranteed greater polishing and greater adhesion of details, especially the eyes, which were designed with shells or obsidian. Some of these masks were made of clay, and could adorn statues or even mummies, serving as a death mask. "Human beings were anonymous members of a group in which human features were often reduced by masks to almost geometric shapes, or were hidden behind tubular noses", says Charles Phillips in the work *The Aztec and Maya World*. Charles Phillips adds that Teotihuacan artists were responsible for producing "depictions in murals, clay objects, masks, and figurines that showed little interest in naturalism and much in religious symbolism".

These details, in turn, were achieved both by carving statues and other forms in stone, and by painting. The scenes depicted could contain glyphs, which suggests a much less sophisticated writing system than that used by the Maya.

THE RELIGION OF TEOTIHUACAN

The most important deity in all of Teotihuacan, unlike neighboring civilizations that always adopted male figures, was a female. The Spider Goddess was a creator deity who, according to Teotihuacan depictions in murals and temples, wears a mask with fangs that resemble a spider's mouth. However, Teotihuacan, as it was one of the largest cities and was home to people from different tribes and regions of Mesoamerica, received the influence of the pantheon of these peoples, which in general, resembled each other. The Feathered Serpent god - a great figure in Aztec culture - known as Quetzalcoátl can be found on the city's premises, as well as Chalchiuhtlicue, the goddess of water, and the god of rain and war, Tlaloc.

Offerings and prayers to these last two gods were a constant concern for the Teotihuacanos due to the arid climate of the region, making water one of the most precious and indispensable resources in Mesoamerica. The positioning of the temples was another differentiator for the Teotihuacan religion, as they aligned with the sun on its June solstice, creating a theory among historians and archaeologists that specific dates on the calendar were important to the people.

The evidence of rituals and other offerings buried in and around these temples, as well as sacrificed victims, illustrates the people's concern with praising and appeasing the will of the gods, especially those associated with climate and fertility.

THE LEGACY

Teotihuacan's legacy is memorable. Not only for its great contribution in areas such as architecture, religion and urban planning, but for its influence on other civilizations, whether subsequent or contemporary. Among the most famous on the list of people who absorbed and exchanged references with the Teotihuacanos are the Zapotec, the Toltecs, the Aztecs and the Mayan. The Aztecs, in turn, saw Teotihuacan as the city that possessed the origin of civilization, worshiping it as a sacred site.

THE DECLINE

Some scholars and historians believe that Teotihuacan collapsed after a great fire caused by the invasion of other civilizations, probably coming from the rising city at the time, Xochicalco, between the 7th and 8th centuries A.D. However recent research reveals that the fire only affected structures belonging to the ruling elite, which leads us to believe that the city suffered an internal revolt, which also led to the destruction of works of art and religious sculptures. The reasons for the destruction of Teotihuacan, according to experts, are mainly due to the scarcity of resources and drought. Following the catastrophic event, the city remained populated for over two centuries before it was completely abandoned, thus falling into a systematic and progressive decline.

THE BEGINNING OF THE MAYA

Thanks to a great scarcity of records, both on the part of the Maya who lost them in arson and invasions, and on the part of Europeans who arrived in Central America in search of riches, the dates that underlie the history of this empire are imprecise. Based on the theory that human beings, still undeveloped, arrived thousands of years ago through the ice channels formed in the Bering Strait, the anthropologist and specialist in the cultures of ancient Mexico, Paul Gendrop, in his work *The Maya Civilization*, says that the origins of the Maya came, apparently, from North America. "The people who made up the Maya group apparently came from the western United States, having settled in the southern Maya area in the third millennium B.C.", the anthropologist explains in his work.

The first Maya settlements occurred in areas that are now swamps and mangroves near the Pacific coast. At the time, they were the perfect region to welcome people into their new lifestyle, fixed and sedentary, thanks to the richness of their food. The food variety provided by the fertile lands, the marine life on the coast and the natural growth of fruits and seeds such as cocoa, for example, guaranteed a privileged location for Maya settlements. "The Maya from the coastal plain traded cacao throughout the entire Maya area. Even today, large agricultural businesses dominate the plain", says Jill Rubalcaba, in *Empires of the Maya*.

Thanks to the good location of the first Mayan settlements, it was possible to make a lot of progress with the growth of civilization and the beginning of what would become the Mayan people, as shown by Charles Phillips in the work *The Aztec and Maya World*. "The settlement of Nakbé, in the lowlands of Guatemala, one of the pioneering centers of the Maya civilization, was established around 600 BC [...] In the southern Maya lands, in 1.800 BC, the population of the Pacific coast of the Guatemala zone lived in permanent settlements of 400 to 1,000 inhabitants, which indicates the existence of a chief or leader who controlled the village", Charles Phillips says in his work.

THE DIVISION OF THE MAYA PERIODS

As previously stated, the dates relating to the Maya, as well as pre-Columbian civilizations in general, are imprecise due to the scarcity of records. However, archaeologists and historians have established a modern system for how to study the eras in which the Maya remained active. These major periods were divided into three phases: pre-classic, classic and post-classic. During the pre-classical era, which went from 1200 BC to 250 AD, small agricultural communities began to grow in an exponential and complex way. This phase is characterized by the construction of large monumental statues, the establishment of trade routes - many of which were built by the Olmec - and a possible government system established in order to govern the norms of society.

The second phase, the classic phase of the Maya civilization, which goes from A.D 250 to A.D 900, is characterized by the splendor of the Maya, who had already spread and built hundreds of cities and villages throughout much of the Central American region, supporting the traffic of millions of people.

The last phase of the Maya era was established from A.D 900 to A.D 1524, a date that historians credit with the end of the Maya civilization and the official arrival of the Spanish. In addition to the European arrival and the devastation caused by explorers, some Mayan cities and kingdoms flourished dramatically but without the splendor of other times.

In his book *The First Maya Civilization*, Francisco Estrada says that the Maya, in all their eras, even with the division of their cities and the arrival of Europeans, were still the same people who live today in the regions of Guatemala and the Yucatan peninsula. "We use the term "Classic" to distinguish them from their predecessors, the Formative or Preclassic Maya of the first millennium BC, and from their successors, the Postclassic Maya who thrived until the arrival of Europeans in the 15th century. But these ancestors are, of course, one and the same people as the present-day Maya who still inhabit Yucatan Peninsula, and walk the streets of Guatemala City, Chichicastenango, San Cristobal de Las Casas, Merida and countless villages."

THE CREATION MYTHS

Many pre-Columbian peoples believed that seemingly inexplicable phenomena, such as lightning and thunder, or even the sun, rain and the planet Earth, could be understood if there was the presence of gods and mythological beings in their narratives. This was no different with the Maya. Their rich pantheon was responsible for great deeds, and among these deeds, was the presence of man on earth and their noble objectives as a rational and capable being.

The following legends are shorter versions made based on the records of the Popol Vuh, one of the sacred books of the Maya people and written by one of the ethnic groups of these people, the Quiché ethnic group, which contains, among other things, religious and poetic reports about the achievements, journeys, myths and legends, among other aspects of the rich culture of that people. All the lines described in the legends were written by A. S. Franchini himself, who, in his work *"As Melhores Histórias das Mitologias Asteca, Maia e Inca"*, uses this method to better tell the stories described below.

THE CREATION OF MAN FROM CLAY

The Maya gods, after having gone through the hard work of creating the Earth, the waters and the skies, decided that the time to populate the newly designed new world had already arrived. To do so, they used one of the richest and most powerful magics, that of words. By the power of the word, they created all the animals that we see today in their vastest and most diverse species: from fish in the great depths of the oceans to birds flying on the highest celestial peak.

The gods spared nothing to have the most abundant planet. Land species had their burrows while others had their branches and webs. All species, of any nature, had their refuges to shelter, reproduce and populate the beautiful planet made by the gods.

However, something still bothered the gods even after all the work. The communication capacity of all these species, their grunts, barks, chirps, groans and roars were not enough for the gods.

The deities wanted creatures that could speak, and above all that could praise their creators in the way they deserved because, after all, they knew that "To be forgotten is to cease to exist". The gods argued and argued in order to understand what their creations were saying, but they were unable to get anything out of it. They needed intelligible sounds, clear statements and appreciation that showed all the gratitude they needed.

Angry after so many attempts to teach the animals to speak, the gods screamed in hallucination and anger about the punishment of those poor creatures. "Stop screaming! Say something that can be understood! Worship us, wretched ones! – [...] Because they refused to praise us, they will spend their lives eating each other, and their burrows and hiding places will always be at the mercy of danger!", recounts A. S. Franchini in his work.

Disappointed, the gods returned to the arduous task of creation, this time in search of a creature that could praise them in a dignified way, with words, with a language they could understand. Determined to make a creature more beautiful and more intelligent than all the animals ever created, they were taken by the idea of creating man, and to this end, after much discussion, they decided to make him out of clay.

After watering the earth with water, the gods shaped the men they imagined from that clay. However, in their rush to see their finished work, the gods forgot to give the clay men a neck. Making their heads unable to move sideways, bow or even express themselves correctly, the clay men were permanently left with asymmetrical heads, and a silly, fish-like expression.

The deities' haste also caused them to forget to dry the clay men, causing the creatures to melt in their first steps. The god of hurricanes, in a quick thought, blew the figurines so that they would dry and not die in front of their creators' eyes. The idea, however, was terrible. The calamity generated by the god's power was so great that almost all the clay figurines were dissolved in mid-air by the force of the winds, and those that remained, at the first step, crumbled like dry clods.

After the failure of the clay men, the gods chose to discard the idea of using this type of raw material for the creation of humans. The solution given by the gods to the imperfect clay figurines was to place them in the oceans, where they definitively turned into fish.

THE CREATION OF MAN FROM WOOD

A new divine council was formed and the discussion about

what new material would be used to test the creation of man was heated. After getting nowhere, they cast lots on grains of beans and corn, until the solution came to light. Wood! The gods began to cut branches and carve the wood with the shapes and curves of the first primordial clay figurine. After long periods of work, the gods, in their final touch, carved the hole in the wooden man's mouth.

This one could not have made the gods happier: he had started speaking intelligibly from the moment they finished it. The gods, without even thinking, created several wooden men and women in series and allowed them to reproduce at will, once the creation had finally succeeded.

However, unfortunately, the wooden men and women possessed a quality that immediately caused the gods to become desolate. They only knew how to talk about themselves, forgetting entirely about those who created them. The men of wood also did not have blood or produce sweat. The resin and sap that the gods had left in their bodies thanks to the wood had evaporated, making them the driest creatures in all of creation. Eager to put an end to this failed experiment, the gods chose to exterminate the first Earth population with a lava storm. The fury of Huracan, the god of hurricanes, was such that even the domestic and daily objects of the wooden men came to life and turned against them, in order to stop the destruction ordered by Huracan. Pans, pots, grills, plates, slotted spoons and even pestles came to life and attacked the wooden men to reduce their dry and empty bodies to dust. Many of the wooden men were torn to pieces and the others, the fugitives and survivors, couldn't find shelter anywhere they went.

Thanks to this, they fled to the open and closed forests, causing the gods, in a last act of mercy towards their once beloved creations, to transform them into monkeys and forever inhabit the forests of the world.

THE CREATION OF MAN FROM CORN

After the dismal failure of the men of clay and even more so of the men of wood, the gods decided to make a new attempt at creating the species that would praise them. The new raw material from which men were to be made was corn. To this end, the god of the Feathered Serpent made the animals search for white corn and yellow corn in the most diverse places and the most fissured mountains.

The parakeet, the lynx, the raven, and the coyote, to name a few of the animals, entered the mountain crevices and their hidden depths and brought back the types of corn requested by the god. The gods then ground and added water to the porridge made from corn grains to mold the first men. Four men were made from the corn porridge – Balam Kitze, Balam Akab, Mahukutah and Ik Balam –, and from the first moment they demonstrated their deep gratitude and recognition to the gods who created them, which filled the deities with joy. They were beautiful and perfect and demonstrated not only their gratitude, but their intelligence through words and gestures. They were as wise as the gods and nothing escaped their vision. Thanks to this intelligence they were able to talk to the gods on equal terms, and this was the great reason for the beginning of celestial discontent.

The gods were not interested in having creatures that closely resembled their own image and their own wisdom. As a prevention, they removed a good part of the knowledge they had from the minds of these men. Concerned about men's ability to see, the gods decided that it would not be good if they could see at great distances, and as a result, they put an end to this gift, making it so that only cloudy and blurred forms could be seen, due to a cloud strategically placed over men's eyes. As compensation for the lost wisdom and the removal of their capacity for great vision, men received a gift from the gods who had seemed, until that moment, only punishers. During a night of heavy sleep, the gods placed four women at their sides, one for each corn man, so that they would always be their companions and thus not feel alone.

The decision of the gods was well received by the corn men, who connected with their companions in such a way that, from these unions, the different tribes that made up the Maya civilization were formed.

The tribes, in turn, began their own journeys in order to establish their place and, above all, survive in a land shrouded, according to Maya myths and legends, in constant darkness, since the Sun had not yet risen.

THE JOURNEY OF THE QUICHÉ PEOPLE

After the birth and creation of the four corn men, and consequently the birth of the various Maya tribes, the world was enveloped in a translucent abyss of darkness.

The Sun had not yet risen in the zeniths of the sky and the tribes spread across the Earth under the little light that still existed. Among these different tribes, which gained different aspects according to their directions, there were the mountain people. Led by the four patriarchs of the Maya civilization – the corn men –, the people of the mountains offered several sacrifices to the gods, but after not obtaining any results, they descended on Tula, a local city, to obtain insignia of power, which were linked to one of the lineages of the Feathered Serpent.

There, Balam Kitzé, who was one of the four corn men, met the god Tohil, one of the names of the Feathered Serpent, and thanks to this meeting the Quichés – the name by which the Mayans would later call themselves – along with other tribes, obtained from the god the blessing of fire. While the Quiché people were able to warm themselves without worry, the other tribes came looking for the Quichés to borrow some of Tohil's fire. Without any qualms, the Quichés, on the verge of giving up their fire, saw a messenger from the underworld appear before their eyes. Her name was Xibalda and, in front of the four patriarchs, she ordered them not to lend the fire, as these tribes would need to pay a price to the gods for the right to have the sacred fire of Tohil. Offering precious stones, the tribes returned trembling and with their mouths purple from the cold, begging for fire. However, Tohil, speaking through the Quichés, ordered the tribes to offer as sacrifices the hearts extracted from some of their members.

Thus, the tribes that later received the name Tamub, Olokab and Qaq Chekeleb became slaves of the Quichés as offerers. Of all the tribes, only Qaq Chekeleb did not subject themselves to the god and did not have to pay sacrifices, but they were still accepted and exempted from the duty of offering.

However, all that the tribes saw on the horizon was the morning star (Venus) in dark skies without the long-awaited Sun. Until one day the god Tohil told them that they needed to offer their own blood because that of the enslaved tribes was no longer enough. At another time, Tohil demanded that the four sages pierce their ears, arms, legs and limbs as a proof of gratitude towards the god. Starving, with nothing to eat and with a routine of only sacrifices, the Quichés left the mountains for other lands, crossing the neighboring sea.

How the crossing was made is not clear from the writings of the Popol Vuh, however, the tribes wandered on rocks when passages opened across the seas. After arriving in distant lands and after crossing rivers, forests and gorges, the Quichés finally received the dawn of the great Sun as a reward for all their journey and worship.

THE SEARCH FOR FOOD AND THE PLAN AGAINST TOHIL

Even though they were blessed with sunlight and the presence of the representation of the star king, the Quichés went on pilgrimage again, since the only things they could feed on were larvae and wasps. Thanks to the scarcity of food and the little water they had, when they passed by a tribe, they kidnapped people who were alone or walking together and sacrificed them to Tohil, leaving the mark of their sacrifices on the roads in skulls next to jaguar tracks. The tracks were fake and made only to deceive the leaders and their tribes. When they found out, a revolt began against the Quichés, but Tohil sent very heavy rain so that the footprints were erased and they were unable to locate the god's proteges.

However, with much cunning and perseverance, some members of the tribes afflicted by the Quichés managed to locate the tribe that had killed so much in the name of their god Tohil, and that had left nothing to the other tribes except a trail of death and bones. The Quichés were seen on the banks of a river that reflected the image of their god, as they bathed without worry, and the tribal chiefs were warned of the sacrificers' location and devised a plan to eliminate them.

To this end, two of the most beautiful virgins of the tribes were selected by the chiefs to offer themselves and have sexual relations with the members of the Quiché tribe, and when they let their guard down, they should lure them to the place where the warriors who would punish the sacrificers were located.

Following the plan, the maidens went to the riverbank and there they found only three young boys who had the names of Quiché gods (it is not known for sure whether they were really the gods or just men of the tribe). These young men asked the virgins what they were doing there. Hesitantly, the virgins removed their clothes and insinuated themselves naked in such a way that the doubts immediately ceased in the minds of the three young gods. Tohil, whispering, alerted the other two gods of the two girls' intentions. The young gods then refused to fornicate with the ladies when they realized their plans. The two virgins, on the other hand, cried in tears asking the young men for mercy and explaining that if they did not fornicate with them, they would be killed upon returning to their tribes.

The three young men then, in conversation with the four wise men, gave the girls clothes with insignia painted by the Quichés, proving that the young women remained in the company of the sacrificers, and sent them away. When they arrived at their tribes, the two young women were met with a barrage of questions from local chiefs, wanting to know everything that had happened. After the young ladies told, in a deceptive way, the finest details about their adventures, the chiefs were amazed at the Quichés' clothes.

Undressing the young women, one of the chiefs put on the first mantle, made with the image of jaguars, and thus paraded through the tribes. The second parade was with the second mantle, with images of eagles. However, on the third mantle with the images of wasps and hornets, the insects came to life, and bewitched, killed the chief of the tribe, stinging him all over his body. Thus the plan against Tohil ended in vain, with the god taking cunning revenge on those who intended to defeat him.

THE TRIUMPH OF THE QUICHÉS

Even after the triumph against the rival tribes in the episode of the two virgins, the god Tohil and the Quiché tribe were still targets of persecution and attacks while they roamed the lands in which other tribes lived. Without any further cunning plans, the enemy tribes of the Quichés, in a council, decided to go to open war against the sacrificers, and without any further waiting or hesitation, they headed towards Mount Hacavitz, where the usurpers of hearts were. Carrying shields and arrows, the enemies had to spend the night in the open field, unable to reach their usurpers before nightfall. However, the Quichés descended silently and, sneaking under the cover of the night like a pack of jaguars, took from the sleeping enemy warriors all their possessions and all their metal, but leaving them alive.

Overflowing with rage, the enemies walked towards the mountain and came across a furious Quiché army, which in the distance was lined up and adorned with all the weapons and metal stolen from them.

However, the Quiché soldiers decorated with metal were nothing more than wooden figurines made by the sacrificers in order to deceive the enemy. Pulled and controlled by the Quiché, the figurines moved as if they were made of flesh and blood. The four corn men and their wives, as well as all their children and descendants, were at the top of the mountain and had prepared traps in jars full of wasp nes tsto fight against their enemies who, eager for revenge, set out to climb the mountain despite the sight of the quiché "army" of figurines.

When they reached the top and saw that the warriors were just figurines, it was already too late, as the real Quichés threw wasp traps at them, which, furious, savagely attacked their enemies, who received stings all over their faces, in their mouths, tongues, windpipes and noses, as well as in their lungs, until they fell into the abyss of the mountain as far as the eyes could not reach them. With the victory, the Quiché people settled on the mountain of Hacavitz, where they multiplied and prospered. After a long time, the four sages passed away and left only a roll of swaddling clothes with an object inside, like a sacred relic to their people.

After the choice of the Quiché leaders, who had brought from the East on a long journey some insignia of power from Tula - place of origin of the corn men - in addition to the Tula writing, the death of the sages occurred. Their wives also died soon after, and the offspring of the four original couples prospered in the mountains. In fact, the mountains in which the Quiché and their descendants prospered are countless, according to the Popol Vuh.

Temple located in Tula

2

SOCIETY AND THE POLITICAL SYSTEM

WHAT LIFE WAS LIKE FOR THE INHABITANTS IN THE VARIOUS KINGDOMS OF THE VAST MAYA EMPIRE

A cultured and literate civilization, the Maya built the foundations of their people not through union in a single empire, like their northern Aztec neighbors, but through diverse commercial connections and the creation of centers that would later become city-states. "Unlike the Aztec people, their neighbors to the north, the Maya never unified into a single empire. Instead, they built commerce centers that grew into city-states (cities that function as separate kingdoms or nations) ruled by kings. These kingdoms formed alliances with one another one day, only to turn into sworn enemies the next.", tells Jill Rubalcaba in the work *Empires of the Maya*.

Even though they were interconnected by commercial exchanges, the Maya often saw each other as rivals, which resulted in wars and the capture of prisoners. However, all this instability did not prevent the Maya from becoming one of the three greatest civilizations in the Americas and one of the most mysterious and developed peoples in the world. Among their achievements are the construction of elevated roads that served as commercial routes, a complex legal system that operated with open-air courts, a broad system of commerce that was the main characteristic of several city-states, in addition to advances in the fields of literature, astronomy, mathematics and medicine. During the rise of the Maya civilization in the 8th century, around 60 independent kingdoms spread across the Maya area, as well as hundreds of small villages and towns.

THE SOCIAL PYRAMID

At the top of the Maya social pyramid were the kings and rulers. Royalty was responsible for being the interpreters of the wills of the gods, ensuring that everything went according to plan in the rituals and, consequently, being treated themselves as figures who approached the divine. Below the kings was the nobility, which was made up of a very powerful social elite, which could only exercise prestigious functions such as administrators and high-ranking public positions, military commanders and priests, in addition to being the vast majority of traders in articles of luxury. Architects, artisans, warriors, artists, farmers and workers of all types, as well as smaller-scale merchants appeared as the middle layer of society and carried out professions that were a decisive factor in the expansion of cities. The citizens considered common people were the peasants who carried out all the heavy work and practically constituted the base of the Maya social pyramid, being above only the slaves and prisoners of war, who were used as a discount on the taxes collected from the conquered regions.

THE PRIESTS

Religious positions were among the most important in all Maya social strata. Equal in power to the nobles, the priests often performed active and privileged roles, such as participating in councils that directly assisted local chiefs and kings. The main priest among the Maya was the Ahuacan, which means "Serpent Lord" and were the final authority in religious and priestly matters, mainly linked to astronomy, divination, writing and conservation of the various information gathered in the books, as well as their interpretation of the sacred books, as well as festivals and rituals to be followed. Younger priests were given the name Ah Kin, which means "Servant of the Sun". This priest was given the task of checking, discovering and interpreting the prophecies associated with the 13 Katunes that were repeated in a cycle.

The Chilanes, which means "Declaimers", were the priests responsible for passing on to the fearful listeners of the Maya people the prophecies, sentences and warnings of the gods, as a kind of oracle. "These men were shaman-diviners who reported on the reality they discovered during spiritual journeys, or in religious visions inspired by mind-altering drugs", says Charles Phillips in the work *The Aztec and Maya World*. Four assistants, called Chac's in honor of the Maya rain god, held the victim's body while it was placed on the sacrificial stone to have its heart ripped out by another type of priest, the Nacom, who was in charge of everything related to sacrificial practices. Nacom's role was fundamental and one of the most honorable. The office of being the skillful executor of the gods was held by these men throughout their lives. "Since the beginning of sedentary life in Maya lands, priests have specialized in knowledge of astronomical cycles and the changes of the seasons. They became the experts of that time, maintaining control through repetitive models of religious life, setting dates for festivals and being the repositories of dynastic history", asserts Charles Phillips in his work.

However, the most important priestly positions, such as high administration, were hereditary and passed on only between the different generations of nobles. Maya priests trained their own children or the children of the most important nobles in the office and the high priest could only be succeeded by his own son or a blood relative. "In Maya lands, the children of farmers, artisans and traders generally could not opt for the priesthood", adds Charles Phillips in the work *The Aztec and Maya World*.

WORK ORGANIZATION

Among the Maya, work was organized primarily by class. Simple men were responsible for working in the fields and plantations, while others went out hunting. For noble and middle-class men, their work was done in administrative buildings in functions of the current king's government, as well as in their workshops, producing valuable pieces for trade and exchange for goods and the like.

Diego de Landa, a Spanish friar who came into contact with the Maya, in his book *Yucatán Before and After the Conquest*, describes Maya work as a collective and continuous effort on behalf of the people and all those who helped. "The Indians have the excellent custom of helping each other in all their work. At the time of planting, those who have no people of their own to do it join together in bands of twenty, or more or less, and all labor together to complete the labor of each, all duly measured, and do not stop until all is finished", the Spanish friar states in his work.

Women had the role of housewives. They looked after the gardens of the houses, as well as the dogs and turkeys that were raised. They also performed manual labor, mainly making fabrics and clothing items to be sold in local markets. However, women who were daughters of nobles and who had a quality education in Maya schools held prestigious professions, such as scribes, for example, which placed some women in Maya society in a privileged role.

EVERYDAY LIFE

Maya daily life was filled with a lot of work on the part of the majority of the population, which was made up of peasants and common people. The day started very early for the Maya and Mesoamericans in general, who always got up before dawn. The alarm clock of the people of Central America was Venus, which honored its nickname as morning star. When it appeared in the sky, it gave the signal to some officials in the Maya cities, who sounded trumpets, to wake everyone up. "Most would get up before dawn, take a steam bath, eat corn to break their fast and then head to the fields, workshops or other places of work with some 'tortillas' on hand to eat later", says Charles Phillips in the work *The Aztec and Maya World*.

Most men, when not working in some middle-class profession as artisans or warriors, worked in the fields and hunted for hours. The women remained at home, spinning, weaving and taking care of everything so that their husbands arrived home and the food was ready. When they finished their grueling workday, the Maya returned to their homes at dusk and ate the most abundant meal they had in their diet. "Some reports suggest that workers, hungry after their shift, ate up to 20 tortillas during dinner", Charles Phillips says in his work.

After dinner, they lit their houses with torches made of pine, and if they were willing, they carried out some more manual work before going to bed, to continue their long working day the next day.

THE HOUSES

The typical Maya houses of the common people were extremely simple and built on an earthen platform or on some rubble. The nobles had buildings in the same format, but more sumptuous and on higher platforms. "Maya homes were built for sleeping and as shelter against heavy rains and flooding. The Maya people built their homes on top of platforms made of stone and tamped (packed down) earth. The platforms were about two feet high – high enough to keep residents dry during floods-with steps cut into the rise", tells Jill Rubalcaba in the work *Empires of the Maya*.

Maya buildings were made with stone walls and clay or adobe blocks that, built around four posts, provided support for a roof made of sticks or straw. The average height of a house was 10 to 16 feet, that is, about 3 to 4.8 meters. "Sometimes only the lower half of the wall was made of long-lasting materials, such as stone or adobe, and the upper part was made of straw or reeds. The house had one or two rooms, if that", Charles Phillips says in the work *The Aztec and Maya World*.

This roof could also be made of flat leaves and with a really high angle of inclination, which made it easier for the roof, even with simple and not very resistant materials, to be waterproof.

Builders generally planned to build three or four of these

buildings side by side in order to build them around a central courtyard, which families could use as a common area. "In some regions, a family group could use several small buildings distributed around a central courtyard. In one, they stored food, tools, and materials; in another, they slept; another was used as a living room; in another, there was the sanctuary and in another, they installed the workshop to manufacture stone tools", explains Charles Phillips in his work.

At the back, the houses had a private part, where sleeping structures were built using branches and young trees. Rugs served as mattresses and they covered themselves with cloaks to avoid the cold at night. Some Maya villagers could use holes dug in their homes, called Chultuns, to store food and water in times of need.

THE FAMILY

Maya families lived in harmony. Even though they didn't spend much time inside the houses, which were only used for sleeping as all the work was done in the open, the families all lived in community. Families also remained together in various tasks arranged in central squares and courtyards. One of the activities consisted of taking care of the house's garden, which could yield good fruits, vegetables and other foods to be used in the Maya diet.

On some occasions, and depending on the region, to strengthen family ties, some women and their children went to the fields to accompany their husbands and stay with them in the corn fields. Besides strengthening relationships between families, this also provided a better harvest. Sometimes houses were built next to plantations for these two purposes.

PREGNANCY AND BIRTH

Pregnancy in Maya times was a blessing and received various types of care. When a pregnant woman was going to give birth, Maya midwives prayed to the goddess Ix Chel, so that the deity would bring a healthy baby and ease the pregnant woman's pain. After the prayers, the midwife mixed plants and herbs and produced an ointment that had anesthetic and sedative functions, so that the mother could relax.

THE MAYA BABIES

For the Maya, the birth of a baby was a source of pure joy.

As they were incredibly superstitious about the hour, minute, and day of birth on the calendar, priests were called upon to determine the baby's strengths according to the birth data. "Babies were named after the day on the 260-day calendar on which they were born. [...] the Yucateco-speaking Maya gave each baby four names: one was chosen by the priest, accompanied by a divine ceremony; the next one was the father's family name; then came the family names of the father and mother, together, and finally, a nickname or family name", states Charles Phillips in his work.

THE RITUAL OF THE ELONGATED HEADS

There was a very important tradition among the Maya, which to this day still fascinates all scholars and those curious about the culture of these people, which was the habit of lengthening the skulls of newborn babies, practiced for a long time among the Maya. The "olive heads", as seen in paintings of several Maya pyramids, were achieved thanks to two boards that, tied to the front and back of the babies' skulls, compressed their little heads to give them the desired shape. One of the possible explanations for this ritual is that the heads should resemble that of Yum Kax, god of corn, who himself had an elongated head, similar to a corncob.

MAYA EDUCATION

Learning in Maya lands was no different from that used by other empires such as the Incas, for example. Maya schools were intended only for nobles and the elite, and the art of writing was taught, in addition to the functions of good rulers and high-ranking administrators. "the majority of the Maya were illiterate. Education was a privilege reserved for the elite. schools run by priests and nobles were for the children of priests and nobles. Those who showed promise and were well-connected continued their studies by learning sacred skills—astronomy, mythology, and divination—for performing religious rituals", says Jill Rubalcaba in the work *Empires of the Maya.*

Young men were taught ritual dances, fighting techniques and military strategy. Women, daughters of nobles and kings were also allowed in the highest professions - the presence of princesses was not uncommon. However, if the schools were purely male, parallel centers were created for these young women.

The education of the less privileged and common people was done at home. The children of the poorest Maya people learned their parents' trades in order to ensure their families' livelihood.

MEN'S CLOTHING

Men's clothing was simpler than women's. Commoners wore a codpiece made of cotton approximately five fingers wide, the fabric of which was called "ex". The most elaborate versions of these fabrics, with feathers, geometric designs and heads of gods, were used by the nobility, who often wore a belt in which they had jade plaques of a god or masks made of the same material.

The rulers, on the other hand, wore sandals with long straps and closed heels, decorated with impeccable craftsmanship with images of ancestors and gods. "In Maya lands, commoners, nobility and royalty wore the same basic clothing, although the wealthier had much more elaborate and ornate versions.", Charles Phillips says in the work *The Aztec and Maya World*.

THE MAYA MARRIAGE

Women wore looser clothes, also made from cotton. These dresses were called huipil, and in some communities it could be a waist-length blouse, together with a skirt, and in other communities it could be a very wide dress skirt with openings for the head and arms. Bishop Diego de Landa had written in his reports to the Spanish crown that Maya women, at the time of contact with Europeans, used a simple skirt and a not very sophisticated cotton garment to cover their breasts. Sometimes they might also wear something underneath their huipil, or skirt, with a shawl over their shoulders. "Today, there are still Maya women in the mountains of Guatemala who wear this huipil blouse. Each community has its own different embroidered geometric designs", adds Charles Phillips in the work *The Aztec and Maya World*.

THE MAYA MARRIAGE

The Mayans were able to marry as soon as they reached puberty. Girls and boys were ready to enter adulthood after reaching this period of life, and going through a ceremony called "the Descent of the Gods". Mothers, after the rites and ceremonies, began to instruct

Maya women with colorful typical dresses, in Guatemala

their daughters in the skills considered essential for a good wife. The ideal wife, in the Maya view, was a woman of the same social level and from the same region as her future husband. The main characteristic of these young women was to always be modest. If they met a man on the way they should turn their backs on him so that he could pass peacefully and unmolested. The Maya wife and woman should also always keep her gaze down and never direct it at anyone else. If she went to the well to fetch water with her cousins or any other man, she should follow this habit.

THE SINGLES

In Maya communities, young men left their parents' home to live in a community building. This building was intended only for these single men, and there these young people entertained themselves with a routine of work and fun. They took prostitutes to the building and paid them with cocoa beans. Unlike married men, who were allowed to have tattoos, single men painted their bodies with black ink to differentiate themselves from those in love.

WEDDING PLANS

The plans regarding the ceremony and the wedding, in general, were the task of a professional matchmaker called Ah Atanzah. The father of the bride could also take on this role. Wedding planning was often arranged between the bride and groom's families when they were just children, by their parents. Families, from the moment their children were promised to each other, began to act as a single family, even if the marriage still took years to consummate.

It was common for families, before making any type of marriage agreement or marriage promise, to consult astronomers-priests, to ensure that bad omens would not haunt the birth dates of both parties, as well as the wedding dates as well. "Marriages between first cousins were permitted, but some unions were taboo. For example, a man could not marry a woman who had the same surname", says Charles Phillips in the work *The Aztec and Maya World*.

THE CEREMONY AND MARRIED LIFE

The nuptial ceremony took place at the house of the bride's father. The mothers of both spouses wove fine clothes to be worn exclusively on this day, and after the wedding the newlyweds went to their new home. The love nest could be a new, recently built house, but it was common for the couple to live in the same group of houses as the bride's family for at least six or seven years. It was also common for in-laws to benefit from the work of their daughters' husbands over this six or seven year period. If the young man refused to work, his in-laws had the right to expel him from his family's group of houses.

After this period, the couple would live next to the bride's father's house. The ceremonies, the marriage routine and the number of wives were defined according to the man's social class. "Commoners had one wife, but richer men could marry several women. Members of the Classic Period Maya elite in cities like Tikal married several times and also had extramarital affairs with concubines", adds Charles Phillips in his work.

DIVORCE AND DEATH

Divorce was allowed in the Maya society and did not depend on social class. One of the most common reasons for this to happen was simple rejection and contempt for the other party or, in other cases, for both parties. The young children of the couple who decided to separate would stay with their mother, or if they were older, they would stay with their father, depending on their gender. "A man could divorce his wife if he demonstrated that she was unable to have children or did not perform certain tasks, such as preparing food or the night bath", Charles Phillips tells us in his work *The Aztec and Maya World.*

If one of the spouses passed away, the other party would have to mourn for a minimum period of one year before they could remarry. Widowers and widows could never marry their deceased spouse's brothers and sisters or even their mothers and fathers. In the second marriage, as the preparation and union rituals were intended only for the first wife, the man who sought to marry another woman would have to visit her house and if she accepted the union, she would have to prepare a meal for him.

3

AGRICULTURE AND ANIMALS

HOW THE CULTIVATION OF FOOD AND RAISING ANIMALS FOR FOOD WAS LIKE

The Maya had the most diverse types of agricultural crops, as they were dispersed over a wide area of land, and their production ranged from corn - their main food - to potatoes, pepper, salt, pumpkin, papaya, avocado and tomatoes. Different regions could produce different foods, since the climate varied from region to region, but each city had its own food base, and thanks to this, the exchange of goods involving food always prospered. Farmers, in turn, were rural men, but because they had a wealth of knowledge in plants, seeds and their sowing, their work was highly regarded by the entire population.

To plant, the Maya used a hollow pipe to slide the seeds in while this same pipe was used to dig the soil. The seeds were stored in a side bag that farmers carried during planting.

THE MAYA DIET

Cities close to the coasts had a diet rich in fish and seafood. The Mayans who lived far from the sea had to be content with eating dried fish, brought by traders on trips. Across Mesoamerica, the main food was corn. Its preparation required a lot of practice and, above all, patience. This is because the corn was first soaked in lime or fresno, and then boiled until its husk and silk came off completely.

After being ground by Maya tools, the corn was turned into tortillas, and could be eaten with chili powder or honey. It was also possible to make corn stews mixed with peppers and vegetables, or even the same meat, depending on the region. "A Maya villager would get up and have corn and water for breakfast; then, he would go to the field with several balls of ground corn stored in leaves. In the evening, after refreshing himself with a steam bath after his field chores, he ate tortillas", states Charles Phillips in the work *The Aztec and Maya World*.

While the Maya nobles had a more elaborate diet, and thus chose the meats and fish they preferred, the poor ate what they could, which most often were home-raised deer and turkeys, birds or other wild animals "The Maya ate deer, home-raised and wild turkeys, iguanas, armadillos, rabbits, caititus (a pig-like mammal), squirrels, porcupines, monkeys, macaws, and other birds, as well as rodents such as agouti, paca and, without a doubt, the rat", adds Charles Phillips in his work.

WATER TREATMENT TECHNIQUES

Around A.D 700, the Maya created their water supply management and containment systems, which could be used for the most diverse types of needs, from irrigating crops to using water as a defense resource. In the Cerros region, for example, drainage ditches were built, which in addition to preventing the soil from becoming waterlogged and flooding, served as defense moats, a type of extra protection around sacred centers.

These projects, in turn, were so massive that they even expended real power. However, they were built by volunteers, as they benefited the entire community, although historians suspect a type of compensation for fees and taxes, as Jill Rubalcaba says in Empires of the Maya. "Some labor may also have been provided by captives, although historians are not sure about this."

In Kaminaljuyú, canals were dug near lakes to irrigate the fields. However, in many areas where lakes and rivers were scarce, the Maya covered and shaped natural depressions in the limestone rocks, called cenotes.

The cenotes were surrounded and outlined with clay, as a kind of outlet for water from these more distant locations or even rainwater, bringing it directly to the Maya reservoirs, using nothing more than the slope of the rocks and the force of gravity. "Tikal's extensive man-made water reservoirs held enough water to provide all the water needs of 70,000 people through a 120-day drought", tells Jill Rubalcaba in the work *Empires of the Maya*.

PLANTS IN WATER TREATMENT

Richly knowledgeable about the natural resources they possessed, the Maya knew how to use plants to their advantage, not only to cultivate land, for food or subsidies but also to help them treat water.

Water lilies were widely used in their reservoirs. This is because the broad leaves of the lilies spread across the surface of the water, thus minimizing evaporation and keeping the water in its liquid state for longer. Furthermore, water lilies can only grow in environments that have clean, fresh, quality water. As a result, the Maya - besides treating the water naturally - could also know when the reservoir was contaminated.

Due to their efficient methods of storing water, droughts were not as much of a problem as floods, which caused waterlogging of the soil on the plains and caused seedlings and seeds to be lost. In drier areas, the Maya used small terraces with compartments in their walls to which they could direct water and retain it.

SOIL TREATMENT TECHNIQUES

If, on the one hand, water did not represent a problem for the Maya, on the other, the land and fields on which they planted depended on a rigorous treatment system so that they would always continue producing. As a technique to conserve the soil and prevent it from turning into swimming pools, the Maya worked their fields so that they were always above the water level, in addition to digging many ditches around them that allowed excess water to drain. "Farmers cut canals in the damp earth and mounded the earth to create raised fields, crossed by irrigation canals", states Charles Phillips in the work The Aztec and Maya World. And he adds: "Many farmers were already growing food in fields created along the Hondo River, in Belize, in 1100 B.C.".

Thanks to the efforts of the Maya in search of their sustenance, it was possible to create life and take food and production from previously unthinkable areas, such as agricultural fields, as Jill Rubalcaba explains in her work: "By applying a variety of techniques to make the most of food production, the Maya were able to spread into areas that had been considered unlivable and even support growing populations".

Another widely used technique was slash-and-burn agriculture, which is called swidden, in which a system of restricted-use clearings is used in which these are burned and used for a short period of time.

This meant that the Maya agricultural fields, on their less fertile lands, could have a useful life of only two to five years. Thanks to this being an aggressive method for the soil, the Mayan fields, after the planting time limit, could not be used for the next five to 15 years, until the soil regenerated.

In the highlands, where thanks to the lava flow and volcanic eruptions the soil became very fertile, cultivation was carried out uninterruptedly, while in the lower and tropical lands, where the soil was poorer, it was necessary to do this kind of slash and burn method on the land. "First they cut down the dense forest with stone axes and then waited for the plants to dry and then burned them to enrich the soil and restore fertility. They could use a field treated in this way for about three years, although then they would have to leave it uncultivated for eight years so that the land could become enriched with minerals again", explains Charles Phillips in the work *The Aztec and Maya World*.

This may also have been, according to the customs presented in the work of Charles Phillips, one of the possible reasons why the Maya were always in exodus from region to region since many farmers who used this method later moved to other locations.

COCOA, THE MAYA TREASURE

Cocoa is the second most important product developed in Maya lands, second only to corn. The Maya took advantage of this natural resource in such a productive way that not only the seeds of the fruit, but the pulp was also used to produce derivatives and the chocolate drink that is widely consumed around the world today. Cocoa and chocolate, in turn, were so important that only the nobility and the highest echelons of the Maya society could enjoy the drink, precisely because it was considered a "drink of the gods".

At that time it was already possible to find the drink in different variations, such as bitter and sweet cocoa, flavored with vanilla essence, cocoa with fruit, cocoa mixed with corn and its exotic form, in which it was mixed with pepper. The Maya drink differs from the current version we consume today only in that the original drink was made with water, not milk.

Among the most diverse uses of chocolate was the preparation of drinks for official celebrations of the nobility and the use of medicines thanks to the calming and toning properties of cocoa. Warriors greatly appreciated the drink thanks to the energy it gave fighters during battles. Furthermore, it was used as an aphrodisiac by newlyweds and as a cream to treat burns, wounds and even rheumatism pain.

BALCHÉ, THE SACRED DRINK

The Maya, like the Aztecs, had a sacred drink called balché. Extracted from the tree of the same name, the drink is made from tree juice and fermented with honey and water, thus having a low alcohol content. Commonly used for religious purposes and festivities, its consumption occurred on a large scale by the Maya due to the need to reach a certain state of intoxication to carry out rituals and ceremonies.

The Maya believed that by reaching this state of intoxication, they could come into contact with forces from the underworld, and with this, they could talk to ancestors, totemic animals and even the gods in order to receive advice and teachings. Thanks to this belief, rituals were always carried out in caves, which gave the Maya the false security that the connection with the underworld would be stronger, since caves are seen as entrances to this lower plane.

Another drink found in Father Diego de Landa's critical descriptions of the Maya habits was chi, a drink made by fermenting the juice of the plant of the same name. Both produced a totally stunning effect and sometimes made the Maya very violent, with even murders occurring after consuming these essences. "The diners drank until a general riot broke out. [...] women were very afraid when their husbands returned home drunk", the friar states in one of his descriptions.

4

THE ECONOMY AND THE TRADE

THE MOST VALUABLE PRODUCTS, TRADED ANIMALS, ROADS AND THEIR SYMBOLISMS

The Maya did not have a currency like we do today, making it difficult to put the Maya economy in quantitative terms the way economists do with modern societies. However, merchants practiced the habit of bartering and even paying fees, which guaranteed the functioning of the Mayan economy. As an emerging class, merchants emerged as an evolution of society.

While nobles shared immense power and influence and were responsible for trading over long distances, others were responsible for shorter routes. There is no specific name for these merchants who carried out their transactions over short distances, however, these small entrepreneurs were responsible for putting a wide range of goods into circulation. In general, these goods were acquired on their travels or even produced by itinerant travelers, who could act as farmers, weavers, potters and tool makers.

THE MAYA MERCHANT NOBILITY

The Maya did not have a network of professional traders like their contemporaries, the Aztecs, but they had a trade that was just as powerful. Subsidized by the great Mayan lords, trade reached levels never before expected in Mesoamerica. Long-distance trade was always carried out by the nobility. Among them there could be rich nobles, or even rulers of some city, which certainly only increased the influence of the Maya elite in relation to other city-states. "At first, the main purpose of long-distance trade may have been to increase the power and prestige of the elite. Exotic gifts were exchanged between royal families, and these cemented relationships. Associations with distant and powerful kingdoms increased a king's status. Rare items from far away glorified the rituals performed by priests and royalty", explains Jill Rubalcaba in the work *Empires of the Maya.*

It is known that in Mayapán, for example, during an invasion, all the merchants and consequently the city's rulers and nobles died during the attack, except for a single survivor who was away for negotiation. "Since ancient times, long-distance trade was dominated by an authoritarian and wealthy elite throughout Mesoamerica", says Charles Phillips in the work The Aztec and Maya World, and further adds: "Trade was the vital element for development".

The power of the nobility as traders was such that these governors could decide on the exchange and distribution of goods, as well as being always present in the creation of laws and other decrees that controlled trade, as Jill Rubalcaba explains in her work: "Rulers of the capital cities controlled trade and the distribution of trade goods. Laws dictated who could wear luxury clothing such as jaguar skins, who could consume special drinks such as chocolate, and which artisans could carve stone monuments".

THE MAYA MARKETS

Maya markets were present in several cities. Located in squares, the markets included a wide variety of businesses that were set up outdoors to promote better movement of people. Some squares were intended solely for this purpose, other squares had areas divided into zones, some for commerce and others for the population, which varied from city to city. "These plazas were designed with trading in mind. Causeways led to the plazas and comfortable accommodations were available for foreign merchants. Just as people do today, the ancient Maya enjoyed their open-air markets. They were not merely places to shop, but also places to socialize and exchange ideas", explains Jill Rubalcaba in her work.

Even though things were, in a certain way, peaceful in the Maya world and especially in its trade, it was not possible to trust everyone. Not all buyers could trust merchants and vice versa. A great example of this was that, for some time, the Maya used cocoa beans as currency. In some circumstances, on both sides, people sold their goods in exchange for this currency, but received very dirty bean seeds instead of the real seeds. Today, this would be equivalent to buying merchandise with counterfeit money.

Cocoa was so valuable as currency that the Spanish explorer and responsible for the dominion of the Aztecs, Hernán Corez, in a letter sent to Spain, explained that the seeds were imported from Maya lands and were not found in other territories and that their exchange power was such that with 100 cocoa seeds one could buy a slave.

However, this cocoa-based exchange currency was not the main point of negotiations, as the Maya could exchange services for goods as well. "A woman might exchange a day of weaving for salted fish. A man might lend a hand building a house in exchange for an obsidian knife", further details Jill Rubalcaba in the work *Empires of the Maya*.

These local markets were one of the reasons Maya cities grew so much. A great example of this growth was the city of El Mirador, which functioned as an important commercial center between 300 B.C and A.D 150.

The merchants and merchandisers of El Mirador had large markets in open squares, so large that many neighbors from other Maya tribes traveled to the city in order to do good business. This, in turn, generated very strong population growth, which led to the arrival of different types of people, who, when working in the city, built some of the most prestigious Maya monuments in history. "A multitude of craftsmen contributed to building this massive metropolis—astronomers, architects, engineers, artists, carpenters, stonemasons, and laborers. Astronomers positioned important buildings to align with the movements of the Sun and the Moon. Builders dressed the buildings in stone and artists decorated them with stucco masks depicting gods and kings", explains Jill Rubalcaba in her work.

Structure located in one of Copán's large squares, which once housed Maya markets

PRODUCTS SOLD

Among the different products sold by the Maya were ceramics, fabrics, feathers, agricultural products, honey, and even slaves. The nobles, for example, always traded the most valuable goods and enjoyed a certain prestige.

"By bringing wealth to the community and trading in select goods, such as feathers, jaguar skins and sacrificial knives – necessary for religious ceremonies –, traders began to enjoy religious prestige", Charles Phillips comments in his work. Cocoa was one of the most valuable products that the Maya could trade. This is because, in addition to its medicinal properties, according to Maya beliefs, it was one of the drinks of the gods, and therefore could only be consumed by a select group of Maya. Another product just as valuable as cocoa was honey. Bees located in Maya regions did not have stingers, which greatly facilitated the collection of honey, which could be mixed with corn and other foods for a richer and more balanced diet.

To ensure a regular supply of honey for the people, the Maya created artificial hives made from hollow logs, which had a small opening for the bees to enter and exit.

Another important Maya product exchanged in their markets was salt. It was produced in large quantities and obtained from salt water from the sea, which was boiled in containers until the only thing that remained was salt residue. White salt from the salt flats north of Yucatán was a favorite of the nobility. Salt producers collected seawater in shallow pans and left them out in the sun. Once the water had evaporated, the salt was collected.

All of these products had different importance, depending on the social classes or even the region in which they were sold. Other types of products that could be exchanged among the Maya were obsidian, jewelry, clothing, and ceramic objects.

MARKET RELATIONS IN MESOAMERICA

The mechanics surrounding exchange relationships in Mesoamerica were not the simplest. Some people possessed resources that others needed and, thanks to this, market relations were always plural and varied. The commercial exchange network was broad and had several mechanisms. To make metates (flat stones for grinding corn), volcanic stone blocks from the Maya mountains in Belize were needed. As for the manufacture of weapons and other cutting instruments, Teotihuacán had a monopoly on green obsidian, a rock of volcanic origin, which in turn was the most prized throughout Mesoamerica.

The Maya in the highlands of Guatemala had control over some sources of obsidian, especially the gray variants, but they did not compare in value with those in Teotihuacán. Jade, on the other hand, was imported in limited quantities from the Motagna basin. The pigments needed to make the Maya artists' paints came from different locations, while the salt came in large quantities from the Yucatan peninsula.

Shells, sea turtle shells, pearls, corals and other marine products were really attractive objects, but they only came from the region where these resources existed. With this, it is possible to have a general idea of how market relations in Mesoamerica and especially among the Maya took place. Each region had its own specific wealth, often making it a monopoly. However, these products were widely traded among the Maya, which left all these resources circulating freely and permanently between the territories of the empire. "Plumes of quetzal, jadeite, serpentine (silicate), pyrite and obsidian were exported from the southern highlands. Jaguar skins and teeth, valuable for their use in ceremonies, were exported from the central lowlands, as were parrot and macaw feathers. From the coastal areas of the southern region, shark teeth, coral, marine mollusks and stingray spines, used to extract blood in sacrificial rites, arrived from the coastal areas, as well as cocoa. Salt was brought from the coast of Yucatán", adds Charles Phillips in the work *The Aztec and Maya World*.

TRANSPORTATION OF PRODUCTS

Transporting these products was a very delicate matter, as most of them were too heavy to be transported manually, and some were too perishable to travel long distances. There is no doubt that Mesoamericans knew the wheel. Researchers have already discovered tiny wheel designs on small wooden toys at Maya archaeological sites. However, the Maya only used it to make toys and other leisure items, thanks to the geography of the region. The unstable soils and steep terrain made it impossible to use the wheel.

Another factor that made life very difficult for the Maya was the lack of transport animals, making the connection between the Maya people and animals more mystical and spiritual than actually utilitarian. "There is no doubt that Mesoamericans knew how to make wheels, as toys with wheels have been found in tombs, but they did not use them for transportation. This was partly due to the fact that they did not have many draft animals and, in addition, many areas of Mesoamerica were not suitable for wheeled transport", explains Charles Phillips in the work *The Aztec and Maya World*. Therefore, chargers were often used. Trained men worked as carriers of goods and constantly traveled in groups to avoid possible ambushes and ensure that products reached their destination. To carry, they positioned the products around their heads or attached to their chests by several ropes, increasing body stability and allowing faster transport with less damage to the materials.

MAYA TREASURES

Just as the Inca clothing was more valuable or as valuable as gold, for the Maya, the treasures were corn and cocoa as the two most important foods, alongside jade and obsidian.

Jade is one of the most used minerals in Mayan arts, whether in the manufacture of pieces and accessories, or simple sculpture. Today, jade is called "the green gold of the Maya," according to historians. "the most valuable substance in the Maya world was jade. [...] The difficulty in working jade, along with the difficulty in finding this rare stone, made it highly valuable.", explains Jill Rubalcaba in the work *Empires of the Maya*. In Central America, jade is found in the exclusive form of jadeite, and it was so rare that the Maya produced pieces by mixing jadeite with greenish stones to give them volume. However, it is common to refer to all Maya pieces with this tone as jade.

Its greenish color is another reason for the high value this ore had among the Maya. "The Maya valued jade fundamentally for its green color, which was the color of vegetation and flowering corn, considering this stone superior, both in beauty and value, to gold itself", tells A. S. Franchini in the work *As Melhores Histórias das Mitologias Asteca*, Maia e Inca. The power associated with this stone could even take on medicinal proportions. A small jade stone could make breathing easier for someone who had difficulty if it was fixed to the person's nose, like a kind of piercing. The

Maya's explanation for this is that the stone gave off a moist, fresh aroma, which aerated the airways and cleansed the lungs.

This stone is commonly linked to a type of refreshment for the soul, thus giving it spiritual powers. Jade also took on spiritual proportions in Maya rituals. It was common for the stone to be used in funeral offerings, symbolizing immortality as it is one of the most resistant materials in nature, and small pieces of jade were often found in the teeth of the dead, to facilitate their entry into the afterlife. Another reason why jade was close to the dead was because of the creation myth: according to Maya beliefs, in the beginning of the world there were three stones at the foundations of the earth, and this gesture was repeated in tombs, with three jade stones.

The jade carved with the figure of flowers represented the ultimate symbol of Maya royalty and placed the sovereign on the same level as the world tree, considering the Maya king as the center of the universe, just as the tree would be.

THE MAYA STEEL

Like jade, obsidian was one of the most fundamental stones in the Maya world. This is because it represents one of the hardest and most resistant materials in all of nature. Today, historians refer to it as "the steel of the Maya." Its hardening came from the cooling of the ores that were expelled from the Earth's crust after countless volcanic eruptions that occurred in eras remote from civilizations in Mesoamerica. "The geography of Central America is characterized, among other things, by the presence of a large number of volcanoes, some of which are still active today", explains A. S. Franchini in the work *As Melhores Histórias das Mitologias Asteca, Maia e Inca.*

The main purpose of collecting and working on obsidian was to make jewelry and objects for rituals. However, as it is one of the most resistant minerals in nature, the Maya also used it to produce weapons of war, such as clubs with sharp blades and spears.

The main deposits of obsidian were located in the highlands of Guatemala, and from there it was transported to different regions of Central America through the extensive Maya trade network.

As it is an ore that does not exist in abundance in nature, other substitutes were used, such as flint, another variety of volcanic rock, which although less resistant, was more accessible to those people.

THE MAYA TRIBUTE NETWORK

Maya tributes are a small portion of what happened in Maya cities, especially in open-air markets. There, the population paid tributes related to commercial exchanges, which in turn were collected by government officials. These tributes were paid in the form of products to the king as a way of thanking him for his support. This habit came from the pre-classic era of the Maya and was a way for the city to raise funds as well. "During the Postclassic Era, lively markets held in the great plazas of the capital cities were sponsored by kings. The king took his cut from every exchange—a kind of sales tax to provide income for the kingdom. Some plazas were just marketplaces, with their own officials patrolling the area not only to keep the peace but also to collect the king's share", tells Jill Rubalcaba in the work *Empires of the Maya*.

The Maya traders who ruled Chichen Itza and Mayapán were responsible for building tributary networks. In Mayapán, products such as cotton, copal, cocoa, honey and turkeys could be used to pay these fees. Another type of tribute was paid by those conquered in war, who could not remain in their posts after being defeated. In payment, the Maya military incorporated the wives of their dead enemies into their own families.

MAYA ROADS AND THEIR CONNECTIONS

To preserve their large trade network and facilitate the exchange of cultures, goods and mobility between city-states, the Maya built a series of elevated paths, known as sacbeob (or sacbé, if in the singular, according to the Mayan dialect). Most paths were built during the Classic Maya era, around A.D 800. Regions like Yucatán, for example, had networks of paths that covered more than 62 miles.

Cobá, another Maya region, was connected to Yucatán and Yaxana by the same 62-mile network and was in a privileged location. There was an intersection of more than 43 paths, and some of them even led to the seaport of Xelhá. "These paved paths facilitated communications and crossings for traders, in addition to solidly strengthening political alliances between cities", says Charles Phillips in the work The Aztec and Maya World. Traditionally, the measurements of these paths were 2.8 miles wide and 1.5 miles high above ground level. The paths could be changed depending on the region, as in the case of Uxmal and Kabah, which maintained a path 13 feet high and over 18 miles long.

The technique used by the Maya to apply cement was surprisingly modern for the time. More than 15 workers pushed a rudimentary five-ton compactor over the paths to finish the surface. "The paths always ran in a straight line and then made a sudden turn to change direction if necessary", says Charles Phillips in the work *The Aztec and Maya World*.

THE SYMBOLISM OF ROADS

The Maya had a deep connection with the sacred, and this was also reflected in the construction of their cities, especially their roads. Cities like Tikal, for example, had a totally enigmatic layout in their configuration: the north was the realm of the supernatural, of dead ancestors who ascended to heaven, and the south was the representation of the underworld.

Therefore, the roads served not only as a connection for the people who traveled through Maya cities but also as a symbolic division between worlds and stories of the richest Maya beliefs. This also explains the placement of the ball game, which was always located between the north and south of the cities, representing an entrance to the underworld. The paths also had the purpose of connecting different symbolic areas and emphasizing the route.

Several remote villages could also benefit from these paths that connected them to the center of the main cities. In a spiral pattern, for example, seven paths of approximately 5 miles led people from residential areas to the squares and the city center.

SEA AND RIVER TRANSPORT

Sea and river transport was also, along with roads, one of the main routes for transporting goods and supplies between cities and towns. They featured extensive savings in terms of time and product conservation, thanks to the speed they provided. Meat, everyday products and perishables could only be sold in nearby markets. In this context, the use of canoes to transport food allowed them to reach further. Communal underground cisterns and adobe barns with thatched roofs, a vegetation cover constructed of reeds and palm leaves, were used to store corn.

In general, the Maya used small boats made of wood with raised edges, called pirágua. There were three main routes within Maya territories. Two of the main trade routes were the river and the sea. The first connected the lowlands of El Petén through several channels, and the other followed the coast of Yucatán. Geographically located in a strategic position between the markets and raw materials of Central America, and with nearby Mexican locations such as San Lorenzo, Teotihuacan, El Tajín or Tenochtitlán, the Maya played a preponderant role in long-distance trade flows.

FISHERMEN AND THEIR TOOLS

The Maya who lived on the coast and in areas that supported fish farming had the function of fishermen and had a variety of fish and other sea creatures that were part of their people's diet.

Among the most commonly consumed seafood were fish, shrimp, lobster and some shells. In other Maya regions, fishermen were responsible for catching mollusks and snails, as well as frogs, in rivers and lakes. The fish were preserved salted, so that they could be transported to distant locations and sold there, lasting for years. Such foods were a delicacy greatly admired by the foreign elite.

The Maya were also responsible for creating, in a series of artificial lakes, some fish farms in which different types of freshwater fish and mollusks were introduced into channels, which could also be located in fields so that the surplus could be fished. Both on the coast and inland, in freshwater rivers and lakes, fish and shellfish were an important part of the Maya diet. Among the techniques used to capture these fish were nets, which carried small ceramic weights at their ends so that they had enough strength to hold the fish.

Fishing rods were also used with hooks made from bones at the end of their lines. After the Postclassic period, the Mayan began fishing with hooks made of copper with bait on their ends.

After a good day of fishing, the Maya would thank the gods, especially the gods Ah Kak Nexoy, Ah Pua, Ah Cit, and Dzamal Cum, who were the respective fishing deities.

HUNTING TECHNIQUES

Maya hunters varied their hunting techniques depending on their prey. To hunt deer and jaguars they used spears, bows, and arrows, or even traps with rope mechanisms, generally to ensnare the animals. To capture crocodiles and other larger animals, such as manatees, stronger nets were used. To capture quails, spiders, monkeys and other animals of the same size, blowguns were used, an instrument with which the Mayans were extremely skilled. From the blowguns, small and fast clay balls were launched to kill monkeys, macaws, raccoons and other animals that lived high in the trees.

To hunt armadillos and tapirs, the Maya dug holes and covered them with branches to disguise the traps and confuse the animals. Traps were also set to capture turtles, iguanas and macaws. Although the Maya were excellent hunters, for them, spilling the blood of animals was a mortal sin. Therefore, the Maya always begged the gods for forgiveness after spilling their blood.

IMPORTANCE OF ANIMALS

The Maya had a profound relationship with animals. Mysticism begins with one of its main gods, Kukulcán, who is the Maya version of Quetzalcoatl, the Aztec Feathered Serpent goddess. Eagles and birds were very important. The main Maya bird was the quetzal, which was traded for its feathers. Anyone who killed a quetzal in the Maya world was punished by the death penalty.

Dogs were also appreciated by the Maya. Just like the Aztecs, the Maya had a supernatural dog in their mythologies, and this dog could freely move through the dark paths of the underworld, as if it were a kind of Cerberus from Mesoamerica. In Greek mythology, Cerberus is the guard dog of Hades, with a monstrous appearance, with three heads, who guarded the entrance to the underground kingdom of the dead, letting souls enter, but never leave and tearing apart mortals who ventured there. The Mayans did not keep herds of cattle or flocks of sheep, and the dog was their only domesticated animal. They also lured turkeys and deer with corn to facilitate their hunting.

Snails, like butterflies, were revered by the Maya as a symbol of death and resurrection, thanks to their spiral form. Bees and fish were also highly respected within Central American indigenous beliefs.

5

CRIMES AND LAWS IN THE MAYA WORLD

THE LAWS THAT GOVERN SOCIETY, THE PUNISHMENTS FOR CRIMES AND THE WARS

Punishments for crimes and laws in Maya society varied according to the class to which the accused or subjugated person belonged. Laws were extremely differentiated between the common people and the nobility. This system, which applied double standards, did not make judgment and life in society fairer, but rather highlighted class differences within society itself and made it clear to which position people belonged, highlighting the differences between different groups.

Within Maya society there were different types of laws. Laws for violent crimes, laws for robbery and theft, and even clothing laws. If, for example, a common person were caught wearing jewelry made from shells or jaguar skin, they would be severely punished, as these were exotic treasures reserved only for the use of nobility. In most cases, if the crime was light and reversible, such as a robbery, for example, public officials held a hearing with the parties involved to resolve conflicts peacefully.

SPANISH INVENTION

Many experts are unsure whether Maya laws actually existed or whether they were invented and retold differently by the Spanish when they came into contact with Amerindian culture centuries ago.

This is because most of the laws described in historical documents date back to post-classic times, when the Maya were already moving towards a more isolated culture, and to this day it is not known whether contact with the Spanish changed any of these real references experienced by the Maya.

PUNISHMENTS FOR CRIMES

Punishments for different types of crimes also varied according to social class. Nobles received lighter sentences than common people. However, depending on the crime, the penalties applied to these nobles were somewhat drastic. If a noble murdered a slave, the noble was barely punished, and his crime was nothing more than a minor transgression in Maya society. However, if a slave killed a nobleman, it was a very serious crime and punishable by the highest penalties.

In the case of theft and dishonesty, the punishment for nobles was much more intense than for commoners. "For example, if a commoner stole something, his punishment was to repay the person he stole from. If he could not afford to do so, he became a slave until the debt was repaid. But if a nobleman stole, his punishment was to have his entire face tattooed. One look and it was clear who could be trusted and who could not", says Jill Rubalcaba in her work.

Punishments varied not only according to the person's social class, but also according to gender. In the case of adultery, a woman who cheated on her husband was punished with public humiliation and shame, while a man was punished with death. Death was an appropriate punishment in the case of adultery, arson, or even rape. However, the victims' families had the right to participate in the judges' decisions, and therefore could demand other penalties instead of death, such as the payment of compensation, for example. If a husband or wife did not want their spouse to be punished, but rather to be forgiven, they had the power to do so. Still, the death penalty was one of the different solutions to crimes.

Death could be applied by throwing a person off a cliff, by strangulation or even by crushing their head with heavy objects such as stones and rocks. The intention, in the latter, would be to break the culprit's neck or crush his skull. In the case of violent crimes, the defendant was stoned to death, shot with arrows or mutilated. Criminals could be ritually sacrificed or murdered in the same manner as their original crimes. In all cases, city officials were the judges. The victim and the accused appeared in front of the judge, who was supposed to remain impartial even when receiving gifts, which were commonly given to these authorities. They were responsible for applying appropriate penalties to each type of person and declaring who was guilty and who was innocent. The mildest sentences were applied to milder crimes and, in general, a simple short haircut would make a person be looked at differently by others, especially among women.

SOLDIERS AND THE MAYA ARMY

Similar to Aztec culture, the Maya army was made up of common men, as nobles were entrusted with administrative tasks or higher positions within the military hierarchy. Farmers, fishermen and other men who had already entered military life made up the ranks of the Maya armies, which varied according to the location of the city-state. Among the Quiché Maya who lived in the highlands of Guatemala, common people were left out of high administrative and government positions. However, it is important to make it clear that the Maya had their armies and carried out their military incursions, just like all the different peoples of Mesoamerica at that time, but the expansion of their territories occurred more through trade than through armies.

TO MILITARY ARISTOCRACY

It was common for rich merchants to be part of the government and nobility due to their great power and influence, in addition to the constant travel that was necessary to carry out their activity. The Maya aristocracy also received fundamental roles within the government and the administration of Maya society, which could sometimes be reflected in the exercise of other functions, such as chiefs and military leaders, priests or rulers. In the classical period, the high nobility of Maya cities was made up of high-level military personnel, administrators and merchants.

The nobles were called Ahauab, and were seen as the descendants of the Quiché founders. Far from any type of mythology, this aristocracy originally came from the putune Maya traders who migrated from the Mexican lowlands, close to the Gulf Coast.

However, these functions and the classification of these military aristocrats were based on their ancestry. Organized into groups according to their ancestry from a common father, the Ahauab gave rise to rulers, military leaders, priests and administrators.

BATTLE CLOTHING

Battle clothing was defined according to position within the military hierarchy. In general, military clothing presented great mobility for warriors, given the need for them to have wide and free movements. Maya soldiers fought in troops and were dressed simply to achieve the necessary mobility. To do this, they used cotton t-shirts and codpieces. Occasionally they wore capes.

Nobles and warriors of higher rank used other types of adornments that reinforced their social status and power within Maya society itself, such as helmets with plumes and jade jewelry. The king, who among so many illustrious figures on the battlefield represented the supreme commander, went to war in the finest clothes, which could vary in elegance, such as a jaguar tunic, which was the symbol of Maya royalty. However, the king seemed to be a more decorative character than a truly combative one, in addition to being protected by elite fighters.

THE LEGAL AND MILITARY HIERARCHY

The Maya military force and political systems were governed by a series of officials who, in turn, obeyed a hierarchy of posts, just as in modern times, to establish the order of command on the battlefields and in the cities. The head of the military was called Sahal and was normally appointed by the king of the city-state himself, who placed someone he trusted in the position, such as a close relative. As previously described, the king was responsible for appointing, according to his wishes, which members of the nobility would be the military leaders, who would be responsible for supervising the payment of taxes and who would be the judges. It was common in Maya society for the king to appoint his relatives, nephews, cousins and brothers to the highest positions, keeping everything in the family. Local judges, and also rulers, were called Batabs. Each Batab governed through a council of two or three men. Decisions on regional issues would only be approved unanimously.

As judges, they maintained a careful routine and constant monitoring of the tributes paid to the king. They were accompanied by two or three helpers who were called Ah Kulelob, who made the society do their bidding. As personal advisors, the Batabs worked closely with a nacom, a nobleman who served as a military expert for a period of three years. The position was high-ranking and highly respected, which required some stricter rules. During this period he was required to lead a sober and celibate life, without contact with any woman, and even those who served him must be men.

Another legal and administrative position that received a lot of attention was the position of Ah Holpopob, a sort of council house that brought together a series of experts knowledgeable about the foreign world and its interaction with the Maya. Daily affairs and other discussions involving small villages or even the trial and investigation of small crimes were carried out by the Tupiles, who would be the law enforcement officers responsible for these small places.

It is important to make clear that these were not the only functions within the Maya legal and military hierarchy. Secondary functions or even those that do not have many records were also performed. For example, services such as speaker or reception officer - who would be a type of ambassador in charge of receiving important foreign visitors to the Maya kingdoms - have already been identified.

Representation of a Maya battle made by a folk group in Mexico

6

THE MAYA RELIGION AND ITS GODS

AS IN MANY OTHER ANCIENT CULTURES, THE
MAYA WERE POLYTHEISTIC AND BELIEVED
THAT EVENTS WERE CONNECTED TO THE GODS

As in many ancient cultures not only in Mesoamerica but also around the world, the Maya practiced polytheism. The Maya people worshiped many gods and goddesses and believed that various natural phenomena and other events were connected with this mystical pantheon. They believed in the divine meanings of all natural phenomena, in a sacred universe whose rules had been established in sacred times.

It is known that in prehistoric times the inhabitants of those regions had as their first cult the worship of the fertility of the land. The inhabitants of Central America fashioned female clay figurines, which were considered representations of an archaic fertility goddess. Later, the Maya and various sister cultures in Mesoamerica gave divine meanings to all phenomena, which led the Maya to worship different gods and goddesses who governed phenomena that could turn against them, and in a destructive way, like earthquakes, for example.

Due to these catastrophes, life in Mesoamerica was lived intensely, and the relationship with the world took a special level. The forces of nature were seen as an invisible, changeable energy that even passed through the veins of human beings. Rocks, trees, mountains, the Sun, Moon, stars and all living creatures, even human beings, possessed a sacred essence and invisible power, at different levels. The Maya believed that this sacred essence that animated everything and everyone was directly connected to us through blood. K'uh (which means sacredness) ran in human blood, which made it a sin to shed blood other than in rituals to the gods.

THE MAYA GODS AND THEIR CLASSIFICATION

Before modern historians were able to decipher the various Maya glyphs, the figures of the gods seemed uncertain and aroused curiosity and confusion in the minds of researchers who were unable to put names on the creatures of the Maya imagination. The solution of scholars at the time was to name the gods according to letters. The letters, in turn, followed the modern Roman alphabet and still serve today as a reference for cataloging and discovering new deities.

ITZAMNÁ

Main deity of Maya mythology, Itzaminá is the ruler of heaven and earth, creator of writing and the calendar. In the Mayan language, Itzamná means "lizard house".

Unlike other gods from other mythologies, nothing is said about violence or war in relation to Itzamná. He was represented as a bird in the sky, or as an old scribe on earth, and the Maya collected the dew for their religious ceremonies thinking it was the tears of Itzamná.

According to archaeological research and discoveries, Itzamná was known as "Lord of the Heavens, Night and Day" and according to legends, he was the inventor of religious rituals, writing and books.

His appearance is described as that of a stooped, long-nosed and toothless old man who had the gift of writing and sometimes adopted a benevolent temperament. Some descriptions state that Itzamná was cross-eyed and had square eyes and sunken cheeks.

Many legends cite him as the creator of the universe, in which he took the form of Hunab Ku. Another type of avatar that Itzamná assumed was that of Kinich Ahau, and it is said that in this way he could transform into a celestial jaguar.

Hunab Ku is considered by some researchers to be the father of Itzamná and is considered the primordial god of all existence. However, it is not clear whether this idea was fabricated by the Spaniards in order to introduce the Maya to the concept of a supreme god and creator of everything.

"Even without there being any reference to Hunab Ku in pre-Columbian sources – the oldest one only appears in the 16th century –, the thesis of the 'single god' was disseminated by missionaries and, in modern times, embraced by followers of the called 'New Era'", says A. S. Franchini in the work *As Melhores Histórias das Mitologias Asteca, Maia e Inca.*

On some occasions, Itzamná appears in the form of a falcon or a serpent. It is common to confuse the snake with a dragon, as it has wings and two heads. One of them symbolized life, associated with the rising of the Sun, and the other, death, linked with the setting of the Sun.

One of the ways to honor him was by collecting the dew from the trees and the accumulation on the leaves and using the nectar as sacred water in religious rituals in honor of him. Part of this tradition was born because the prefix itz of his name means "dew" in the Quiche language. However, itz could also mean the sacred spirit of all things.

Itzamná was married to Ixchel, the goddess of the Moon and the rainbow, and had - thanks to their sacred marriage - four children. These children were called Bacabs and remained spread across the four corners of the world. The task of the Bacabs was to sustain the heavens, in addition to helping the Maya with climate and agricultural predictions. In some cases the Bacabs could also cure illnesses, although much of the work was done by their father, Itzamná. It was not uncommon for Maya gods to have several different roles and functions.

CHAC

Chac is one of the most important gods in the Maya pantheon precisely because he controls one of the most fundamental and necessary elements in the life of the entire Maya society: rain. It is commonly interpreted as the Maya version of Tlaloc, one of the most prestigious Aztec gods.

"Chak is one of the oldest Maya gods. Carvings on stelae from 2,200 years ago show Chak performing dual roles. On one stela, Chak is portrayed as the kind rain god bringing rain from the sky and fish from a river. On another, Chak is the aggressive warrior god swinging his ax", says Jill Rubalcaba in the work *Empires of the Maya*.

In most figures, Chac is represented with two enormous tusks and an abnormally long nose, which is sometimes mistaken for an elephant trunk. Chac also had scales and fins. The rain god was often depicted wielding a lightning, an ax or a serpent. Part human, part reptile, he had scales on his body, as well as long tusks and snake-like whiskers.

The ax carried by Chac was the universal symbol of thunder. With that same ax, legend has it that Chac beat a serpent full of water that he carried on his back. A god linked to agriculture, Chac often demonstrated his strength. Once, when he saw the men begging for food, he drove his ax hard into a mountain, splitting it in two. From inside the mountain, a large quantity of corn cobs emanated.

Chac, like most of the gods of the Maya pantheon, unfolds into more than one figure, being able to take on different appearances which, in turn, were modified according to the color of his representation. The Maya believed that each Chac avatar represented a cardinal point, and that each point had a color. For example, the eastern Chac is red while the western one is black, the northern one is white and the southern one is yellow. Thus, each specific Chac was blamed when floods or destructive torrential rains occurred, for being "angry". Still, Chac is considered by the Maya to be a benevolent god in most cases.

One of the ways to calm the rain god was to perform sacrifices in his name in places considered sacred to this deity, such as cenotes, which were aquatic caves that the Maya believed were related to the god, but which were actually just natural landslides.

Sculpture of Chac, one of the oldest gods of the Maya civilization

YUM KAX

Cousin of the Aztec god Centeotl, Yum Kaax is nicknamed by the Maya as the lord of the forests and the god of corn, being one of the most popular gods recognized by the Amerindian people, as corn was the main food of the Maya culture.

It took on an even greater proportion because the gods used the food of which Yum Kaax is the guardian as the base material to mint man and forge him to become what he was in Maya society.

The deity is represented by a slender young man who carries an ear of corn on his head. The elongated spike aspect was also presented by the god's head itself, which represented a great standard of beauty for Maya culture. Sometimes the figure of the god appeared severed, in the best Mesoamerican style, as life and germination were linked to death, inseparably. With this, a strange practice was carried out in honor of Yum Kaax. People took their own blood with thorns, placed it in medium-sized containers and deposited it at the door of their homes. The Maya believed that, by leaving blood at the god's disposal, Yum Kaax would guarantee a good harvest and would grace the people so that they would never lack corn.

KUKULCÁN

This god has a unique importance within Maya culture because he is the god of the Feathered Serpent, one of the main deities of Mesoamerica and who, in Aztec culture, is represented by the god Quetzalcoatl, whose name has the same meaning. Benevolent deity, legend has it that after falling into disgrace in the city of Tula, where he was a very powerful king and priest, the Aztec god Quetzalcoatl migrated to lands under Maya rule, where he settled in the form of Kukulcán.

"This version, however, is problematic, since the two feathered serpents differ radically in temperament, because while Quetzalcoatl – at least in his Toltec incarnation – presents himself as a peaceful god and enemy of human sacrifices, Kukulcán Maya reveals himself to be a warrior god and promoter of bloody hecatombs", says A. S. Franchini.

Chichén Itzá was one of the Maya cities that received the most worship services to Kukulcan. At this time, during the 10th and 12th centuries A.D., the Toltecs invaded Maya lands and put into practice the cult of the morning star (Venus).

Even associated with the planet, the god was one of the oldest deities in all of Mesoamerica and received different names, such as Tohil or Gukumatz, for example. Still, many scholars have doubts about the element that Kukulcán governed. Some claim that Kukulcán would be the god of the winds and several legends are based on this knowledge. Others already place the wind as an element that would be an extension of the domains of the god Chac, known as the god of rain by the Maya.

AH PUCH

Ah Puch takes the form of the god of death for the Maya and, as a custom in several Mesoamerican cultures, his figure was represented in glyphs as a skull. Supreme lord of the nine underworlds, he was the supreme god of death and ruled over all the misfortunes of the world. Unlike the good-natured Itzamná, Ah Puch is a frankly malevolent deity, the creator of misfortunes that always culminate in the greatest of all, which is death.

His description matches his face. Its trunk and limbs were covered in dark-toned flesh and sometimes full of spots, which resembled a decomposing body. His back and ribs were completely exposed, while ornaments made from snakes tied his hair and were used as necklaces.

KIMI

Acting as another god of death, Kimi was always represented as a small god with a repulsive appearance and with amorphous characteristics, such as an abnormally enlarged belly. The god became extremely popular in the post-classical period, although some scholars still have doubts about who this deity was. The Maya credited him with an evil but simple personality, who could be easily deceived, as the twin heroes did when faced with the gods of Xibalba.

Sacrifices were offered to this god, as well as to all infernal gods, but in particular, this god received the K'ex sacrifice, which was made with the victims' hearts or even with babies. The latter were always represented in ritual paintings inside temples with jaguar features. These were-jaguar babies were directly inherited from the Olmec culture, which also offered them to their deities.

In any case, after the arrival of the Spanish, this god fell into disrespect and ridicule by the Europeans, who called him Kisim, which means "Flatulent One" in Spanish, thanks to his fetid breath associated with the putrefaction of bodies and death.

Kisim was the god of death and decay and lived in the underworld. It was drawn by the ancient Maya with only the bones of the ribs, skull and teeth exposed, without any flesh, or with putrefied flesh, wounds and a swollen belly, in allusion to a decomposing corpse. His head was adorned with strings filled with eyeballs forming crowns, or serving as bracelets or anklets.

It was common for this god to walk with his faithful mascot, an owl. Owls were considered creatures of the underworld by the Maya because they hunt at night and have the ability to see in the dark. Maya legends describe owls as messengers that fly between the underworld and the human world.

IXTAB

Ixtab was one of the most revered and popular Maya goddesses in the heyday of Mesoamerican society. The only difference she had from the other gods was that she was not the goddess of any natural element, but of suicide. Part of this popularity came from the fact that people who commit suicide were part of a class of people with a privileged status in the Maya paradise.

Suicide in Maya times was much more common than in modern times, thanks to this belief that the person who commits suicide would have a superior and blessed existence alongside the worshiped gods, which made this act not a way of escaping the unpleasantness of earthly life, but of reaching a higher level.

Killing oneself was considered a noble act and worthy of the highest rewards within Maya society, but the author of the noble act had to collect his reward from the other side. Very little is known about the goddess of suicide, thanks to Spanish efforts to destroy several Maya records. In the Dresden codex, for example, it is possible to glimpse the deity hanging from a gallows, with a round spot on the face and closed eyes, symbolizing death and putrefaction.

It is no surprise that this goddess was also associated with the death god Ah Puch as his wife.

VOTÁN

Votán, whose original name was Oolt'an Balam, means in the Quiche language "Jaguar who speaks from the heart", and was one of the most feared gods in Maya society because he was associated with the underground world and consequently with earthquakes.

It is important to make it clear that thanks to its distinctive name and the neglect of various European and Spanish authorities when coming into contact with Maya culture, its name has been confused several times, even being associated with Norse gods, as A. S. Franchini says in his work. "One of the favorite 'workhorses' of defenders of the thesis of Viking colonization in the Americas is this authentically Maya god, whose original name, Oolt'an Balam ('Jaguar who speaks from the heart'), came to resemble, by mere chance, to Wotan, the Germanic version of the Vikings' Odin".

Votán became known thanks to the friar Ramón Ordoñez y Aguilar, who reported the god in his work *Theologia de las culebras*, in which the disappeared Maya title *La probanza de Votán* is mentioned.

Among the deity's most incredible feats is the founding of Palenque, one of the most important Maya cities of all time. It was believed that Votán supported the Earth on his shoulders while he was hidden in the depths of the world. Earthquakes were a consequence of their arduous burden. While supporting the planet, from time to time the god moved, which caused the seismic shocks that the Maya knew and feared.

EK CHUAH

Called by the Maya "Black War Leader" or "Black Scorpion", Ek Chuah is one of the most cited gods within Mayan codices and was responsible for some of the greatest calamities that changed the world. One of these calamities was promoted by Ixchel, the goddess of floods, with whom he joined to promote the destructive character of the work. He usually appears black, which for the Maya would be the color of war, and with his lower lip hanging down.

Among the most common representations of the god, he has a long scorpion tail that always rises when the deity stands on bent knees, in a battle position. One hand carried a shield and in the other, he raised his mighty club made of flint. Unlike most deities, Ek Chuah is not governed by Manichaeism, but is also endowed with a constructive and useful face, expressed in the figure of patron of cocoa and god of merchants and travelers, resembling a peddler, carrying a burden on his shoulders.

IXCHEL

This goddess was also associated with natural elements. Generally identified by her association with the Moon, love, weaving, motherhood and even medicine, Ixchel was the goddess of the rainbow.

Even linked to all the elements that represented benevolence within Maya society, the goddess also had her dark side, when she was also associated with floods. Some Maya legends state that this goddess was also responsible for the flood that caused the extinction of one of the suns of previous eras. When associated with disasters and floods, the goddess is described by the Maya as an old woman with a sour and disgusting countenance, who pours the contents of huge skins (bags made of pig skin to retain liquids) onto the Earth.

Her resemblance to the god Coatlicue, another Aztec deity, was tremendous due to the fact that she wore a cap made of a serpent on her head. Her fingernails and toenails were shaped like claws, like those of the jaguar, another creature that is part of Maya mythical imagery, and her skirt had human bones as ornaments.

Often, within the Maya imagination, the goddess also took the shape of a rabbit, as she was always associated with the Moon and its craters resemble the shape of the animal. According to legends, the goddess Ixchel would also be Itzamná's wife and thanks to this her disagreements with the god were constant. The separation of Ixchel and Itzamná was not the most peaceful, and it is said that the god left his wife one-eyed in a cruel fight, which would explain why the moon shines less than the Sun for the Maya.

According to beliefs, both ascended to the heavens, Itzamná in the form of the Sun and Ixchel in the form of the moon. The island of Cozumel, located on the east coast of the Yucatán Peninsula, houses one of the most famous places of worship of this goddess.

BULUC CHABTAN

Just like Ixtab, Ah Puch and Kimi, this is another god with an unpleasant nature in the Maya pantheon, who was used on several occasions to justify atrocities involving prisoners of war and sacrificial victims. Buluc Chabtan is considered the god of violent

Representation of Ixchel

death and bloody hecatombs and was created to honor the practice of human sacrifice.

His representations in statues and glyphs present him as a merciless god painted all red, while holding a large human heart in both hands. Among the various stories of Buluc Chabtan, the god entered houses together with the goddess of death Ah Puch to set fire to homes with a torch.

It was thanks to this god that the priests, in their sacrificial rituals, painted the bodies of stunned victims and tore off their hearts, smearing themselves with blood and elevating the human muscle towards the stone idol and the Sun.

HURACÁN

In the Quiché language, Huracán means "One-Legged" and was considered one of the most important gods in the Maya pantheon, having taken part in the creation of the world together with Kukulcán and, therefore, being one of the creator gods described in the Popol Vuh. Like other gods who were responsible for more than one type of element, in addition to creation, Huracán was considered the god of storms, and according to the Madrid codex, his name was the word adopted by the conquerors to name the hurricane.

"Huracán, however, was not only the god of storms, but also the god of fire, and it was he who, combining his gifts, destroyed the first human race through a lava storm", says A. S. Franchini in his work. With a long nose and a mirror on his forehead, his appearance resembles that of the Aztec god Tezcatlipoca, which means "Smoking Mirror" to the Aztecs.

Mesoamerican syncretism made them both, at the same time, gods of creation and destruction, since thanks to their physical and elementary characteristics, they were often associated with both, being a symbol of winds and storms.

XAMAN EK

One of the most beloved gods of the Maya, the Xaman Ek was the "God of the Polar Star" and was responsible for guiding and showing the way to several merchants and travelers who traveled the Maya roads in the dark. Xaman Ek is associated with the north cardinal point, which is the polar star, the favorite star of travelers. This is because in the skies of the Maya peninsula, this star barely changes position throughout the year and remains clear at night, serving as a guide to travelers.

With a strange appearance and no resemblance to the stars, the god is described by the Maya as having a monkey-like face full of black spots and a wide, disproportionate nose. Even with his peculiar appearance, the god is benevolent and is not related to anything degrading or bad. He is mentioned several times in records as being linked to nature and being, in some cases, accompanied by the rain god, Chac.

7

MAYA WRITING

EXTREMELY COMPLEX, IT WAS ONE OF
THE MOST DIFFICULT FOR RESEARCHERS
TO DECIPHER

Maya writing is, without a doubt, one of the most complicated in the world and one of the most difficult to understand. It is possible that in Maya society only a quarter of the population knew how to read and write. Despite this, many knew how to interpret the inscriptions and what they represented, even without having had formal teaching in reading and writing. "[...] many others could admire the artistic achievements of the ah its'ib while the meaning of the words was explained to them. Among the elite, being literate was a matter of pride", says Charles Phillips in the work *The Aztec and Maya World*.

The decipherment of Maya writing is so problematic that it was considered, even in the middle of the 20th century, as an insoluble problem. Today, artifacts such as sacred stones, stucco, wood, codices, garments and even pottery can be found containing the Mayan language throughout Mexico, El Salvador, Guatemala, Honduras and Belize. The Maya writing system and language, even though it was a challenge for the 20th century, is now on the way to being fully deciphered. Approximately 75% of all known Maya texts can now be read fluently by experts.

THE ORIGINS

The origins of Maya writing are still imprecise, however, the hieroglyph system was developed several centuries ago and even before the splendor of the Maya, by civilizations such as the Olmecs. The Olmecs, in turn, as developers of one of the oldest writing systems in all of Mesoamerica, used literal images, that is, pictographs, although some scholars claim that the Olmec system was completely developed in their time. "Scholars can not say with any certainty where and when Maya writing began. But this does not mean that writing was imported from elsewhere", says Jill Rubalcaba in the work *Empires of the Maya*.

In fact, the Maya system had its first steps with writing, dating back to the middle of the pre-classic period, which approximately corresponds to the year 300 B.C. As time went by, the system became more complete and sophisticated, being added to several monuments. One of the possible explanations for the lack of evidence that points researchers to a precise date can be seen in the work of Jill Rubalcaba, *Empires of the Maya*, in which she explains that the Mayan word for the verb "write" comes from the verb "paint." Therefore, if the Maya's early efforts to develop their writing system were painted on surfaces and then washed, this would explain the lack of physical evidence for the evolution of Maya writing.

MAYA GRAMMAR

Maya grammar evolved over time, and many scholars claim it was an evolution of Olmec grammar. The Maya grammatical system is composed of hieroglyphs that can be pictographic (representing real objects or actions), or symbols that represent an action (and which can also indicate adjectives, prepositions, plurals or numbers).

However, there are phonetic hieroglyphs, which combine sounds. Others indicate an idea or a concept and, in this case, the Mayan language resembles some Eastern languages. There are more than a thousand different symbols in Maya writing, and in just one paragraph between 300 and 500 symbols can be found. Although there are only five vowels and 19 consonants in the Mayan language, there are more than 200 types of syllabic combinations to form words.

UNWANTED TOUCH-UPS

The Maya did not just write on materials that could be easily destroyed or that were perishable. They wrote in caves, on stelae (stone or column erected with inscriptions), on buildings and even in the pyramids, which today carry vivid memories in the various glyphs left by those people.

After researchers like John Lloyd Stephens and Frederick Catherwood carried out their field research and copied the drawings onto their drawing boards, countless other researchers came looking for the forgotten wonders. Therefore, it is necessary to pay attention to the drawings, as many of them were retouched by artists and many drawings collected on-site passed through the hands of researchers who were willing to "enrich" the original material. One of the most striking cases is that of the Count of Waldeck. Studious and eccentric, when making copies of Palenque's paintings, he added some "decorative glyphs" on his own, in addition to suppressing other details, which left the original work with non-existent and totally unreasonable elements.

THE MASS DESTRUCTION OF DIEGO DE LANDA

When Diego de Landa (1524–1579), a friar serving the Spanish crown and the Catholic church, arrived on the Yucatán peninsula in 1544, both the natives and the Spanish royal family themselves could not imagine the extent of the destruction that man would cause. Diego de Landa came to the "New World" to catechize and evangelize the natives, thus having no authority for anything beyond that. However, when he came across Maya writings and their representations of the various gods in glyphs, temples and other places, he was horrified. Obsessed with establishing cultural cleansing and completely erasing the customs and rituals of the natives, Landa propagated the idea that Maya books spread pagan beliefs and thus destroyed, during the years he was present in Central America, every copy of literature he could find.

The hunt for books was such that works containing information about all Maya research in the fields of medicine, astronomy, mathematics, as well as historical works about the cities and their rulers, were destroyed. "Landa burned more than 5,000 Maya images and dozens of Maya books that he believed to be works of the devil. Books written by the Maya about medicine, astronomy, religion, and history were all burned", says Jill Rubalcaba in the work *Empires of the Maya*.

After his witch hunt in the king's new lands, the monarch himself condemned the actions of Diego de Landa and ordered him to return to Spain to be tried for the abuse of power used by a simple friar of the Catholic Church on the native Amerindians. During his trial, however, he was found innocent after a series of defenses made based on the work *Relación de las cosas de Yucatán*, in which the friar himself describes, through his observations, the Maya people and their culture, customs and beliefs. "Although Landa was responsible for erasing the Maya's own historical account, he is also responsible for much of what is known about the Maya today. His information was based on his own observations and extensive interviews with the Maya people he met. Still, it is important to remember that the book was written by someone who respected what the Maya had achieved but was angered by their religious beliefs", says Jill Rubalcaba in her work.

This anger felt by Diego de Landa can be seen in his work, which shows all the hatred felt by the friar in his detailed reports about Maya culture: "We found a great number of books in these letters, and since they contained nothing but superstitions and falsehoods of the devil we burned them all, which they took most grievously, and which gave them great pain", says the friar himself in his book.

The friar returned to the Yucatán peninsula with the title of bishop of the region in 1573. However controversial his attitudes may have been, his book brought important records about the Maya lifestyle and society at the end of the pre-Columbian era.

PROHIBITION OF USE

After the great destructions carried out by friar Diego de Landa in the name of his religion, the Maya were prohibited from using such writing and dialects due to the fact that they were "works of the devil" and should be extirpated from the culture of the natives. Therefore, many of those who survived the Spanish hunts and who had some knowledge of writing or ancient dialects were prohibited from passing on their knowledge, and thus, much of the literary and linguistic culture of the Maya was lost. Maya writing was prohibited from being used by natives, who would be punished with the death penalty if they circumvented this prohibition.

THE VARIOUS CODICES AROUND THE WORLD

After the great persecution of Diego de Landa and the destruction of almost all Maya books and their most important customs, rituals, habits and culture, some texts were found that survived the fire. All texts were documents dating from the post-classic era and were written with Mayan hieroglyphs. They were all sent to Europe as souvenirs and kept as curiosities by explorers.

Today, these books are called codices and, in total, there are only four of them in the entire world. They were named after the European cities where they are currently located: Dresden, Paris, Madrid and Grolier.

THE DRESDEN CODEX

This codex ended up in the hands of German researcher Alexander Von Humboldt, who immediately became interested in the fascinating Maya writing and its exotic signs. It arrived in Europe first through Austria, until arriving in Dresden, Germany, a city where it remained under the researcher's care.

The Dresden codex was made by flattening a long, thick sheet made from tree bark and then applying a light lime paste to the sheets to lighten them. Folded in the format of an accordion, the long sheet of the codex contains in its 74 pages many of the Maya teachings compiled in almanac format, with mathematical tables and medicinal information, as Jill Rubalcaba tells in her work: "The book was constructed by folding the long sheet accordion style to create 74 pages. it contains almanacs, mathematical tables for eclipses, predictions about floods and when to plant, as well as information about sickness and cures", explains Jill in the work *Empires of the Maya.*

The book was one of the four remaining, and like the others, its role was fundamental not only in gaining knowledge about Maya culture, but also in deciphering the signs and symbols of Maya writing. Humboldt's investigations have led many scholars to become interested in Maya culture and research the monuments full of secret inscriptions to this day.

THE MADRID CODEX

The only codex made after the conquest of the Spanish is the Madrid codex. Exhibited and preserved at the Museum of America in the Spanish capital, it has already attracted several scholars to decipher its 111 pages and 56 sheets, painted on both sides. This made researchers believe, for a long time, that they were two independent manuscripts, known as Troano and Cortesianus until, in 1880, French researcher León de Rosny concluded that they were a single parchment.

Michael Coe, a scholar on the subject, concluded that it was produced after the Spanish conquest, thanks to evidence of recycled paper among its bark paper sheets, coming from the Tayasal region, a Maya region that remained independent until 1697. "The Madrid codex combines details about Maya beliefs regarding the four cardinal points and the deities that presided over them, with information about New Year celebrations and detailed almanacs of the 260-day calendar. Like Grolier's codex, it appears to have been written hastily, or by a inferior scribe, as it contains grammatical errors and careless handwriting", reports Charles Phillips in the work *The Aztec and Maya World.*

THE PARIS CODEX

The Paris codex took its name from the French capital and has been kept at the Bibliothèque Nationale since 1832. According to historian Bruce Love, the codex was probably produced in 1450, in the Itzá city of Mayapán. Preliminary laboratory analyzes show that its 11 pages were written by just one scribe, unlike the Dresden codex, in which it is possible to identify five to eight different calligraphic styles on its pages.

Among the various information contained in the small manuscript are the katun cycles (periods of 7,200 days) and the period of 13 katuns (somewhere around 260 years). Gods responsible for the katuns and the Maya time periods can also be identified. The Paris codex illustrates 13 constellations, represented by mystical animals that carry the glyph of the Sun in their mouths. The arrangement of the constellations resembles the signs of the zodiac as we know it today. This codex revealed to the priests much of the knowledge discovered about the universe.

THE GROLIER CODEX

The Grolier codex is dated to A.D 1230, and according to researchers and laboratory tests, it is the oldest of all four codices discovered. It got its name thanks to the event of its release, in 1971, when it was exposed for public viewing at the Grolier club, in New York.

The codex has a group of ten pages, which should probably make up a much larger group of writings, with at least twice as many pages. Painted on one side, the pages were written with very little care and in a hurried manner, indicating an inexperienced scribe and a possible unsuitable environment for the work. "It contains little information beyond details about the signs of the days and the deities associated with each phase of the planet's cycle. [...] An explanation of its origin suggests that it was discovered inside a wooden box along with a sacrificial knife and a mosaic mask, in a dry cave near Tortuguero, in the current state of Chiapas", says Charles Phillips in his work *The Aztec and Maya world*.

THE SCRIBES

Scribes formed an important part of Maya society. In addition to prestige, the scribe should learn to deal with the responsibility of writing sacred texts, and above all, being the guardian of all those texts. The chief scribes of Maya cities, during the classic period, were in charge of administering, caring for and preparing the books of large libraries, which in turn had a very wide variety of works. In these copies, the most diverse texts were kept. In golden times, libraries could contain records on Maya genealogies and descendants, texts on arcane rituals, as well as knowledge on astronomy, medical information and even compendiums on herbs, plants and animals. In the classic period of the Maya society, scribes had the status of geniuses.

Thanks to this special treatment, Maya scribes were educated in special schools close to the royal palace, in the center of the cities. Only descendants of rulers, the elite and nobility could attend this school. The training of the older sons was aimed at military education and power, while the younger ones, children of younger wives or concubines, attended schools and took their first steps in the life of a scribe.

In Maya society, women could also play the role of scribe and it is possible that the schools of the time admitted daughters of nobles and even princesses to teach the art of writing.

THE SACRED BOOK POPOL VUH

Popol Vuh, in literal translation, means "Book of the Council" and the copy known to the modern world is just a copy of the original manuscript that, lost to time, received a fair copy by the Quichés themselves after the Spanish conquest, centuries ago.

The Popol Vuh is nothing more than an extraordinary account, of great imaginative quality, of the Maya world and all its deeds, legends, goddesses and all the religious and spiritual aspects that the society experienced. It is considered the most important literary work of the pre-Columbian Americas, it is the sacred book of the Maya, which brings together all the beliefs of these people who reached their peak during the so-called classic period.

Some experts also believe that, given its importance, the Popol Vuh is the equivalent of the Catholic Bible in Maya society, not in the context of veneration, but rather of respect, as it contains in its pages the Maya myths of the creation of the world and of men, which date back many centuries. An important excerpt from the Popol Vuh chronicles the adventures of Xibalba, a pair of hero twins who travel to the Maya underworld.

In fact, the Popol Vuh was originally written as a large, long poem, the first half of which contained more than 9,000 lines. After the transcription of the Popol Vuh by the Quiché people in 1554 into the Roman alphabet, the book was divided into four parts.

THE PROPHETIC BOOK CHILAM BALAM

One of the most important books and one of the few to survive from the Maya empire - many of them coming from cities in Yucatan - was the Chilam Balam. The most famous are the Chilam Balam of Chumayel and the Chilam Balam of Tizimin. Chilam is the Mayan word used for priests and shamans, while Balam means jaguar. The priests called "jaguar priest" or Chilam Balam, were the most prestigious.

The supposed author and writer of the Chilam Balam Maya texts that are known today, in European language and transcribed from the Mayan language in the 15th century, was a priest. Although, in reality, the Chilam Balam books are credited to several people in different generations, who recorded history before, during and after the Spanish conquest.

The Chilam Balam was a book that kept all the information that the Maya had about prophecies, which the people took very seriously. The Maya believed that the gods themselves revealed this information to the prestigious priests, who in turn received the heavy work of being the interpreters of ancient texts, revelations and sacred calendars. For the Maya, by studying the past they could predict the future, since history was circular and repeated itself regularly.

MYTHS OF THE CREATION OF THE WORLD: CREATION FROM VOID

Amid the stillness and vastness of nonexistence, three Maya gods who pre-existed in this temporal and material void lived fully in a dark and silent sea of nothingness, while the world was not yet created. Kukulcán, with his serpent body and his quetzal bird feathers, was one of those gods who, immersed in the void, delighted in the silence and took advantage of the watery chaos to put their thoughts in order.

Thinking was one of the most pleasurable tasks, if not the main one, among all that they could do, and it was highly valued by all the gods. One day, after spending all their time thinking, the gods decided it was time to communicate with each other. The primordial dialogue was intense, and together, the three decided to create light through three rays, so that all that darkness was banished and they could see what was before them.

So powerful, the gods decided that they needed something more than just light to put an end to the endless vastness that they enjoyed in their time. All that was needed was the word Ulev (which means Earth in the Quiché language). The cry of the word Ulev by the three gods caused the planet Earth to emerge from the middle of the void. Little by little the planet took on the shape it is known today - since before it had valleys and mountains, the Earth was like an empty shape, like a cloud.

Many woods and forests were formed from the union of different vegetation that were created by the gods, one after another. After a good while of work, the gods looked and congratulated each other on their creation.

Mayan hieroglyphs on display at the Grand Museum of the Maya World of Mérida, Mexico

8

BLOOD RITUALS

HOW THE MAYA VIEWED DEATH AND WHAT
HUMAN SACRIFICE RITUALS WERE LIKE

The Maya viewed death in the same way as any other people in the Americas and even other ancient civilizations. They believed that as soon as a person died, their soul ascended to heaven and to a new life in the afterlife. However, even living with the death of thousands of people every year thanks to sacrifices to the gods, the Maya felt as much pain and suffering with the loss of loved ones as modern civilizations feel today.

Charles Phillips tells how, unlike the Aztecs, who even had a celebration for the dead, the Maya felt deep anguish over the death of their loved ones. "The Maya deeply feared death, despite also knowing it well. Far from celebrating those who died, the disconsolate survivors spent days and nights crying and screaming in grief and despair", says Charles Phillips in his work *The Aztec and Maya World*.

However, the custom of crying profusely and expressing anguish and desolation through screams and bellows was only permitted at night. "When a Maya person died, their loved ones cried quietly during the day, but after dark grievers were loud and mournful" says Jill Rubalcaba in her work *Empires of the Maya*. For days, the Mayans fasted in honor of their loved one, hoping that he would make it to the other side safely.

THE PATH OF THE MAYA SOUL

For the Maya, there were two types of souls: the corporeal soul, which was the first soul of the human being, and their "zoomorphic" soul, which was linked to an animal. The first soul, which coexists with the second within the person's body, was called Sak Nik Nahal, which in literal translation from the Quiché language, meant "White Flower" or "The white conscience of flowering". This first soul left the body after death and ascended to the heavens, beginning the dead person's pilgrimage through the underworld, which could take some time before finding its eternal resting place. For the dead person to achieve success on this journey, the living continued to serve him with food or money in the form of jade, which was a form of offering.

The second soul was called "way" by the Maya, and was linked to another living being in this world - animals or a mythical entity - or even natural phenomena such as rain and thunder. "For the Maya, however, the soul was not seen as something opposed to the body, both being part of the universe as a whole. It was seen as a connection with all living things in the universe, and could even take on material and tangible forms, being far from constituting a 'vaporous' and immaterial entity opposed to the physical world", adds A. S. Franchini in the work *As Melhores Histórias das Mitologias Asteca, Maia e Inca.*

HUMAN SACRIFICES

Human sacrifices were extremely necessary in Maya society, thanks to their beliefs. The Maya believed that, by performing this type of ritual, the gods would be merciful and bring favorable measures to the people. "Offerings or sacrifices of blood were important because this was seen as a powerful source of k'uh. For the Maya the greatest source of k'uh was life itself, and by extension, the ultimate sacrifice was offering the life of a human being to the gods. Thus, the most important and meaningful rituals were sanctified by human sacrifices", says Robert J. Sharer in the work *The ancient Maya.*

Other reasons for human sacrifices would be the arrival of a new kingdom or a new ruler, and even the birth of someone important in the eyes of the Maya, as Charles Phillips says. "The Maya believed that human sacrifice was a necessary rite for special occasions, such as the inauguration of a new kingdom, or of a temple or building, or the announcement, birth or blessing of an heir to the throne", explains Charles in the work *The Aztec and Maya world.*

In some human sacrifices, the Maya practiced cannibalism. Although rare, it occurred depending on the circumstance, but generally warriors and military leaders devoured the bodies of their bravest and most courageous enemies with the intention of acquiring the courage and qualities of the dead person. "If the victim had shown courage in battle, the body was cut into pieces and eaten by the warriors and chiefs at the ceremony. The hands and feet were presented to the priests. If the victim was a slave or a prisoner of war, the master or captor kept the bones to wear as evidence of his superior skill", adds Jill Rubalcaba in the work *Empires of the Maya.*

BLEEDINGS AND BLOOD RITUALS

Blood was considered by the Maya as a sacred force, capable of governing aspects of life and bringing joy to the gods when it was spilled, and thus, this was the only acceptable purpose, in addition to punishments, for such spillage to occur. Bloodletting, which was the act of shedding one's own blood, was considered a privilege and it was the responsibility of the elite to grant it to the gods. "The Maya believed that by spilling this most sacred human substance - blood - they could contact the gods and their ancestors", says Jill Rubalcaba in the work *Empires of the Maya*.

Preparation for bloodletting was carried out over days, in which participants had to fast or avoid prohibited foods, remain chaste and without sexual intercourse, in addition to consuming hallucinogenic plants to reach the barrier between the natural and the supernatural.

Victims were pierced with obsidian blades, carved bones or thorns. When these people died, they took the tool to show the gods their sacrifice. Cutting one's hands and pouring the blood into incense containers or an altar was also a form of blood ritual, which took place on special dates in the Maya calendar.

THE VICTIM

Among the Maya, the victims chosen for sacrifices could be the most varied, but in general they were always people outside Maya society or the dying who no longer had a purpose in the eyes of the people. Commoners, who were later converted into slaves if their debts were not paid off or forgiven, as well as nobles, rulers and other generals from rival tribes who lost to the Maya in war were chosen as sacrificial victims.

It was common for sacrifices to be made through execution or self-flagellation, which usually lead to the belief that, like the Incas, the Maya doped and drugged their victims so that they would not feel pain. However, the Maya were more concerned with courage than with pity for their victims, since a frightened victim in fear of death was considered a bad omen. One of the reports made by Diego de Landa, which proves this practice, is that the flagellants did this in droves, piercing their own genitals. "They anointed the devil in this way, with blood from all sides, and whoever did the most was considered the bravest", says the friar's account.

SACRIFICE RITUALS

Sacrificial rituals took place in different ways. In one of them, the victim was painted with a turquoise blue pigment, which was the color of the Maya sacrifice, and they were forced to climb the steps of the temples wearing a pointed cap. At the top, under the gaze of a crowd, the expiatory stone was painted turquoise blue and four of the priest's assistants, who were also wearing clothes of the same blue color, held the victim on the surface of the stone, while the high priest held him and opened his chest, extracting his beating heart. "After that, the chilam stained the statues of the honored gods and his own skin with his blood. He threw the body down the steps to the terrace and there the apprentices skinned it. Then the skin was returned to the chilam, who wore it as if it were a garment and danced in front of the crowd", says Charles Phillips in the work *The Aztec and Maya World.*

Another way of carrying out the sacrifice was with the victim also painted turquoise blue and naked, with a pointed cap, tied to a post while warriors danced around them. The priest extracted the blood from his genitals and offered it to the gods, and finally, the warriors who had bows and arrows interrupted the dance and shot a volley of arrows until the victim fell dead.

CENOTES AND SACRIFICES

One of the most curious aspects about the Maya is that they could associate natural aspects and monuments as a kind of work and sign of the gods. Cenotes, which were natural landslides of limestone soil found in Central America, was one of the places where the Maya believed this happened. True water caves, with deep water wells, were the Maya's favorite places for sacrificial drowning in honor of the rain god Chac, one of the main gods of the Maya pantheon. "Victims were thrown into these drains accompanied by animals and riches, as it was believed that such wells were supernatural portals to the god's underground home", says A. S. Franchini in his work *As Melhores Histórias das Mitologias Asteca, Maia e Incas.*

On some occasions, the victim managed to remain floating for a long time, which forced the Maya to remove the person from the well and apply an aromatic, numbing resin to their body. If the victim survived this second attempt, they were rescued and had to tell the main priests what they had heard from the gods or the underworld during the immersion. If the arguments were convincing, the victim was no longer sacrificed and became a kind of saint or chosen one of the god for the Maya.

In the Chichén Itzá cenote, one of the around 5 thousand wells estimated to exist throughout Mesoamerica and the most famous one, archaeologists have found everything in its depths: from human bones, jade jewelry and gold discs, to even modern objects, such as a dressed doll, which proves the persistence of the cult among the indigenous people.

THE MAYA BURIAL

The Maya had several customs regarding burial and honoring their dead, depending on the time and region in which they were located. Generally in Maya regions, the dead were buried close to their ancestors or even behind their homes.

Wrapped in a shroud, the deceased received several offerings that had a connection with their earthly activities. The poorest and common people received less traditional offerings, such as some precious stones or even their work tools and food, according to Bishop Diego de Landa, in an account recounted by Charles Phillips in his work *The Aztec and Maya World:* "According to Bishop Diego de Landa, the commoner from Yucatán was buried with his cotton clothes and a few grains of corn or jade beads in his mouth, which would serve him well on his journey along the smooth path of the Milky Way towards the lower world", says Charles Phillips.

The richest, generally nobles and rulers, could be buried with a death mask made of jade, with tombs filled with offerings and riches, and more sumptuous burials than the others. "On special occasions, a temple-pyramid was created or an existing one was reconditioned to house the tomb of the dead king", says Charles Phillips in his work.

During the Postclassic period, the Toltecs and their successors, who had extensive participation in Maya culture, preferred cremation, in which the deceased was incinerated sitting and their joints were buried with the offerings.

Maya death mask

9

MAYA MEDICINE

THE CURE OF DISEASES, SURGERIES, MEDICINAL PLANTS AND MEDICAL RITUALS

Originally, as medicine was closely linked to religious and mystical concepts involving the Maya imagination, doctors were priests, shamans who had great knowledge of the region's plants and knew how to treat these problems. Families transmitted this art of healing throughout the generations, in a hereditary way. At a very young age, the child went out with his father, a doctor, to learn about the logic, processes, plants and medicines, as well as the treatments applied to the most diverse patients.

After his time as a simple assistant, the boy grew up and became an apprentice, until finally, with experience and age, he reached the position of doctor. "The Maya doctor was considered both a healer and a prophet of illnesses. They were very careful about public health and the proper use of water and personal cleanliness", says Carlos Rivera Williams in the article *Historia de la medicina y cirugía en América: la civilización maya, published by Revista Médica Hondureña.*

Men and women were considered fit to practice medicine and the art of healing. Men achieved a doctorate more easily than women. While men received the title of "Ah-Men" still in their youth, women only received its equivalent after menopause, as they were "free" from impurities derived from childbirth and menstrual cycles.

THE SOUL OF TREES IN THE CURE OF DISEASES

One of the main beliefs of the Maya, as well as other tribes and civilizations in Mesoamerica, was that not only men, but all of nature had a soul, regardless of whether it was animated or not. This belief was no different with trees. Despite being strongly rooted in priests, since medicine is linked to shamanic practices, they believed that trees could transmit not only positive energies, but also illnesses. The tree infected people through a kind of "flow of energy" similar to a "mystical wind". Thus, whenever someone fell ill among the Maya, the priests would run after the responsible tree.

Once identified, the tree had to be contacted by the priest, who used the most prophetic and shamanic rituals to get in touch with the tree's soul and convince the plant to do no more harm to anyone. Once the "evil flow" caused by the tree stopped, it took a matter of days for the victims of the negative energies to regain their strength and move on with their lives.

SURGERY IN THE MAYA CIVILIZATION

Surgery in the Maya civilization was not used in the way it is today. Dental surgeries were performed not with the aim of curing cavities or extracting teeth, but rather to embed jade stones in fillings, for ornamental and therapeutic purposes.

However, surgery to cure some type of illness was carried out in a rustic way and without much care, not due to a lack of knowledge of the anatomy, but rather of the pathology and hemorrhages and infections, which caused complications that almost always resulted on the patient's death.

THE SWEAT HOUSES

Maya sweat houses were very similar to the saunas that exist today. They were used, among other things, to maintain good hygiene and to relax muscles after a long day of work.

However, they could be used for medicine as well. Pregnant women were constantly sent to the bathroom to undergo a type of prenatal treatment. "Sweat-baths were also used for healing. The Maya believed they were a cure-all for everything from aching muscles to poisonous snake bites", says Jill Rubalcaba in the work *Empires of the Maya*.

Saunas were built of stone and had slightly vaulted ceilings. The state of fervor in the bathhouses was achieved with splashes of water that were thrown onto scalding stones to create steam for healing and treating the sick.

The rooms in the sweat houses also had a drainage system to remove excess water while the Mayans rested and enjoyed the treatment on benches, where they could remain sitting or lying down.

THE CONCEPT OF ILLNESS

The Maya believed that illnesses and all diseases known to them were not a natural cause of exposure to viruses and bacteria, which, through various means of transmission, contaminated everyone. Instead, the Maya believed that diseases were all caused by the gods and sent as divine punishments for some act that displeased the deities, attributing the origins of illnesses to the heavens. "The Maya believed that diseases came down from the heavens as punishment from the gods [...]

Ideas about diseases were closely related to moral and religious conceptions", states Carlos Rivera Williams, in the article *Historia de la medicina y cirugía en América: la civilización maya, published by Revista Médica Hondureña.*

DISEASES

Great experts on diseases, the Maya gave different names to all of them, depending on their dialect and region. Among the best-known diseases were the typical common cold, bronchitis, tuberculosis and psoriasis, which were combined with other types of diseases, generally caused by fungi. There were also sexual diseases among the Maya, such as gonorrhea, for example.

One of the most serious diseases, which today would be equivalent to a possible epidemic in terms of danger, with delirium and convulsions, skin eruptions and fever, was called cocoztli, the name given to typhus or typhoid fever.

The second major disease known to the Mayans - which brought the same danger to them and all the surrounding tribes with its symptoms of abdominal pain, jaundice, sudden fevers and delirium - was the yellow fever.

MEDICAL RITUALS

Diseases were cured by Maya doctors, who could be shamans or healers. Just like modern doctors, they had books made in a precise manner by scribes, which contained references from the medical field. One of the manuscripts that survived the Spanish persecution was the book *Ritual of the Bacabs*. It describes ritual chants for curing various illnesses, such as fevers, parasites, burns, bites, itches and even broken bones. "To cure a toothache, The Ritual of the Bacabs advises the shaman to repeat, "I stand ready to take his fire. I roast him in the heart of food, in the tooth of the green wooden man, the green/stone man. Red is my breath, white is my breath, black is my breath, yellow is my breath.", says Jill Rubalcaba in the work *Empires of the Maya.*

PLANTS AND REMEDIES

Maya remedies were prepared from a series of herbal mixtures known to herbalists, who acted on behalf of the patient in order to combat the various diseases that already existed in Central

MAYAN GLOSSARY OF DISEASES

Common cold - Tzonpiliniztli

Scabies – Ezcazahuatl

Bronchitis – Tlatlaxiliztli

Tuberculosis – Tetzauhcocoliztli

Mycosis – Quaxincayotl

Pediculosis – Ixocuili

Psoriasis and other fungi – Xiotl

Gonorrhea – Nemecatiliztli

Sexual impotence – Totomiauiliztli

Diarrhea – Apitzalli

Hematuria (Blood in urine) – Extlaxixtli

Coated tongue – Nenepiltextli

Pus – Temalli

Heartburn – Chuhual

Indigestion – Balbuthil

Colic – Tabnakil

Dysentery – Hubnak Puuch

Leishmaniasis – Chech

Malaria - Camoackin

America. Some herbs, such as kanlol, which is a strong diuretic found in Maya lands, were used to treat high blood pressure, heart failure, kidney and liver problems, as well as glaucoma.

Some other solutions were made by grinding plants and used to treat problems linked to worms, as a kind of natural dewormer. Others, such as pastes and ointments made from tree bark, were used as a natural repellent against mosquitoes that transmit malaria and dengue fever. "Ointments made from tree barks served as effective mosquito repellents, preventing diseases carried by mosquitoes such as encephalitis (an inflammation of the brain), malaria, dengue fever, and yellow fevers", says Jill Rubalcaba in her work.

Francisco Itama Chorti, a Maya remnant, collected in the 17th century more than 350 medicinal plants used by the ancient Maya in various treatments. Achiote (annatto seed), which was used in different conditions involving the mouth and feet, as well as "chichicamole", whose root was reduced to powder to be used as a very powerful purgative, were some of the examples.

To heal broken arms and other limbs, the Maya applied a special paste called cocopatli to the region, which hardened after a while and was perfect for immobilization and healing broken bones. The Maya's skill in medicine was such that the time to be paralyzed with the hardened paste varied according to the part of the body, but was generally 20 to 30 days.

Another type of treatment used by the Maya was bloodletting. Despite being a noble and ritualistic act, bloodletting could be considered an offering to the gods, since diseases were also caused by them and so it made sense for them to use this method to cure illnesses. For example, if a person had a headache, it was necessary to bleed the back of the neck with small cuts to improve the condition.

10

THE RITUAL GAME AND SPORTS

RELATED OR NOT TO RELIGION, THE MAYA
PRACTICED SPORTS AND EVEN HAD AN
11-A-SIDE BALL GAME

It is not known exactly how many games and sports the Maya practiced. Unlike the Aztecs, who had a wide range of disputes and games involving poles, beans and also the ball game, the Maya were best known for leaving to posterity the large fields in which they played pok-a-tok. "The 'ball game' – tlachtli for the Aztecs and pok-a-tok for the Maya – dates back to very ancient times in the history of Mesoamerica. With the Aztecs it already had at least 2 thousand years of history, as it was already played in Mexico in the middle of the second millennium B.C", says Charles Phillips in the work *The Aztec and Maya world.*

However, scientists believe that the Maya inherited the game from their Olmec influencers and precursors, since the rubber ball used for competitions may have been born in the lowlands of the Gulf of Mexico, a region in which the Olmecs were very developed during the second and first millennium B.C.

THE RULES OF THE GAME

The rules of the pok-a-tok ball game varied depending on the Maya city in which it was played. Among the variables were the number of players, the way to score points and even the members who could touch the ball. In most cases, two teams of 2 to 11 men played with a ball made from rubber extracted from a type of tree that produces latex. The ball measured between 6 and 8 inches in diameter.

The objective of the game was to keep the ball moving, without it falling to the ground or being touched by feet or hands. Players could only move the ball with their heads, hips, elbows and knees. Scoring points was the most complicated part. To score, players had to make the ball pass through an arch on a side wall of the field. However, other forms of scoring were accepted.

"There were stone markers at different points in the playing area, and on some occasions, one could score by hitting them, or sending the ball to the bottom of the opponent's defended zone", says Charles Phillips. The rules varied over time as well. In Teotihuacán, for example, players were drawn by artists on the walls of buildings also holding sticks in their hands, which suggests hitting the ball, as done in baseball games. In Chichén Itzá and other ball fields around the post-classic period, the objective - still not very well defined by historians and scholars - seemed to be getting the ball through the hoops. In other regions, players scored points by hitting the ball at the edge of their opponents' zones.

THE PURIFICATION

As well as for medicinal use, bathhouses were used by the Maya for purification rituals. One of these rituals involved pok-a-tok, and therefore some bathhouses were located close to the game fields.

Saunas were also used as preparation for carrying out sacred and purification rituals, as the steam was believed to expel evil spirits. Purification for the game is closely associated with the mythical background that the ball dispute has with the fantastic tales of Popol Vuh and the epic of the twins against the gods of Xibalba.

THE PLAYERS

Because the game carries great religious significance and is an honor to the gods, the players were brave warriors who represented the battles fought, or even the rulers or the nobility

Detail of one of the arches in the Uxmal field

in general. In other situations, prisoners who were nobles and rulers of other tribes could be forced to take part in the rival team of the home tribe, making the dispute increasingly fervent, despite being unfair, as Jill Rubalcaba says: "The local elites would typically win the game and then sacrifice the losing lord." The custom of sacrificing people, whether prisoners or not, did not happen frequently, and it was often considered an honor to be sacrificed in a ball game, as this way the warrior and player would always have a privileged place in the other world.

"The carving at the Great Ball Court also shows the winning team's captain extending his neck toward the losing team's captain—who cuts off the winner's head. This would seem a poor reward for victory. However, the Maya believed this decapitation to be a sacred honor. Someone killed in this way was granted immediate entrance into the otherworld", adds Jill Rubalcaba in her work.

CHICHÉN ITZÁ AND THE GREAT COURT

The magnificent ball field at Chichén Itzá is the largest in Mesoamerica. Measuring 225 feet in width and 545 feet in length, the playing surface measures 118 x 479 feet and is surrounded by thick walls 26 feet high, with stone arches right in the middle of the entire length. "The oldest fields had marks to indicate the center of the playing area, which divided the field into two equal halves. Some fields had niches at their ends, on diagonally opposite corners", explains Charles Phillips in his work. The fields also often had seats for spectators, which measured approximately 11 inches high and 7.8 feet long, almost like modern bleachers.

The large ball field at Chichén Itzá was part of a ceremonial complex filled with sacred structures, which meant that the city contained at least 13 ball fields, a greater number than any other Maya center. Part of the structures of these camps was made like a large staircase, in which part of the religious ceremony occurred, generally the outcomes and executions of battles fought in the fields.

"Some Maya fields had annexes where there were steps to which the captain of the defeated team was tied as if he was a ball, from where he was thrown to die, to celebrate the god's descent into the underworld", says Charles Phillips in his work.

THE BALL GAME TODAY

Today, the ball game known by the Maya and also by the Aztecs is most practiced in the lands of Mexico. However, the rules have been adapted so that so many players, and above all, sacrifices are not necessary. "a game directly descended from the ancient one is still played in parts of northern Mexico", says Jill Rubalcaba in the work *Empires of the Maya.* Known no longer as pok-a-tok, but as ulama, the game has several variants that are played according to the region in which it is played. In the north of Sinaloa, a Mexican state, ulama de brazo is played. The game takes place between two teams of three people who face each other trying to score points in the same way as the ancestral game, through arches. However, in this variant the use of the forearms is allowed, which are surrounded by thick protection.

Ulama de cadera is another variable of the game that can be found in the south of Sinaloa, and unlike the ulama de brazo, teams are made up of five or more people precisely because only touching the ball with the hip is allowed. "The players can use their forearms but not their hands to hit the ball. The ball is very heavy, so typically, one wants to hit it with the hip. By using the whole body this way, a player can push the ball higher up", says Jill Rubalcaba, still in her work, about some of the variations of the game currently played.

The third variant of the game, ulama de palo, is the one that comes closest to the original described in several temple scenes. In it, players use clubs similar to those described in religious scenes, as if they were wooden rackets. The game, in general, was described as just a memory of the past, until it was revived by small remaining tribes in the Mexico region during the 1980s.

RELIGIOUS FOUNDATIONS

The Maya believed that the game symbolized the fight between the Twin Heroes and the gods of Xibalba, however, this was not the only association the Maya had regarding their sport. Some historians suggest that the ball used in the game represented the Sun itself, thus exemplifying the efforts of the Maya to ensure that the star always remained proud, in the position of giver of life in the heavens. This would also explain the rule in which the Maya could not let the ball fall to the ground. Despite this, the dichotomy between life and death

Religious inscriptions from the ball game at Chichén Itzá

was seen as something real, making the games true reenactments of battles fought between tribes and peoples. "There are scholars who say that the matches meant the narration of battles, and that in the end the captured enemy nobles or kings were sacrificed, in order to conclude the story itself", says Charles Phillips in his work.

THE EPIC OF THE TWIN HEROES

The game in the Maya regions was closely associated with the feats of the twin heroes Hunahpú and Xbalanqué, who challenged, through a ball game, the gods of the underworld and lords of Xibalba. Legend says that there were two men, Hun Hunahpu and Vucub Hunahpu, who bet a lot on games of chance and spent all their time playing ball. The gods of Xibalba, responsible for the most diverse tragedies in the world, invited the two to a game in the underworld.

Arriving in the underworld, the gods began to play several cruel games with the two men. First, they told them to sit on a bench that was so hot they almost couldn't stand it. Then they sent the men to spend the night in the Dark House, one of the regions of the underworld, with just a torch and two cigars to light the place.

Unbelieving that they had spent all that the gods had given them, the deities punished the two by death on the ball field, while Hun Hunahpu's head was displayed on a tree. A girl from the underworld, named Xquic, went to look at the tree, and intrigued by the young Hunahpu's head, came so close that the head spat on her, making her pregnant. She later gave birth to the twin heroes Hunahpú and Xbalanqué. The twins, upon learning that the gods of the underworld killed their father and uncle who loved the ball game, decided to take revenge.

They started playing ball making a lot of noise, which made the Xibalba lords challenge the heroes to a match. Upon arriving at Xibalba, the gods decided to play with their lives, just as they had done with their father and uncle. However, the two passed without difficulty all the trials of the gods and their terrible creatures, inhabitants of the Dark House, the House of Razors, the House of Cold, the House of Jaguars, the House of Heat and the House of Bats. After going through several trials imposed by the gods, the twins played against the deities, and cunning as they were, easily won all the ball games they played.

Furious, the gods of the underworld burned the twins in a large oven, ground their bones and spread the powder across the river. Six days later, the lords of Xibalba were incredulous when the twins reappeared in front of them claiming to have conquered death. Challenged to prove their achievements, Xbalanque ripped out Hunahpu's heart and ordered him to stand up. Hunahpu stood up and the gods believed that the young men had overcome death and discovered a way to revive the dead.

Eager to learn about the experience, the gods asked the young men to rip out their hearts and return them to life. However, wise men, the young men ripped out the hearts of the deities, but left them dead, reducing the power of the underworld and leaving the universe ready for the creation of human beings.

11

MAYA SCIENCE

DISCOVER ASTRONOMY, MATHEMATICS, NUMEROLOGY, COSMOLOGY AND THE MAYA CALENDAR

THE MAYA IN ASTRONOMY

The Maya, like the Incas and Aztecs, had a great knowledge of astronomy. The Maya priests, who with extensive knowledge were responsible for studying the stars, cross-referenced them to determine when the sacred dates were and how the temporal cycles were plotted. "Priests and astronomers kept an incredibly precise record of time, with the movement of the stars as a measure", says Charles Phillips in the work *The Aztec and Maya World*.

The means of observation that Maya astronomers had at their disposal, as well as the various other neighboring peoples of Mesoamerica, were simple and limited the priests to calculating stellar movements with the naked eye, while using marks on pairs of crossed sticks as references. "Sacred buildings were designed to celebrate celestial and seasonal events, such as solstices and equinoxes, as well as to facilitate their observation", states Charles Phillips in his work. A great example of a construction located at a strategic point, not only by the Maya, but as a reference throughout Mesoamerica, would be the Pyramid of the Sun, in Teotihuacán, which is aligned to mark the daily path of the Sun as it travels from East to West.

El Caracol Astronomical Observatory, located in the city of Chichén Itzá, Mexico

Maya calendar: 365 days divided into 18 months that contain 20 days each

The level of Maya astronomy was so surprising, as well as precise and accurate, that their buildings intended to be astronomical observatories are very similar to those we have today. "The Maya, like most peoples, observed the movements of the stars and planets. But the Maya took this science to an extraordinary level by building towers in which to make and record their observations. Caracol, the observatory at Chichén Itzá, looks remarkably like a modern observatory with its dome shape and slits of windows for observing the skies", adds Jill Rubalcaba in the work *Empires of the Maya*.

THE MAYA CALENDAR

The Maya had two types of calendars. The first of them was based on 13 groups of 20 days, which totaled 260 days. It was mainly used to mark ritual dates and religious events.

The second calendar is similar to the modern solar calendar and is based on 18 groups of 20 days, plus five additional days that the Maya believed to be nefarious, totaling the usual 365 days. This calendar was used by civilians, unlike the ritual calendar, used by priests.

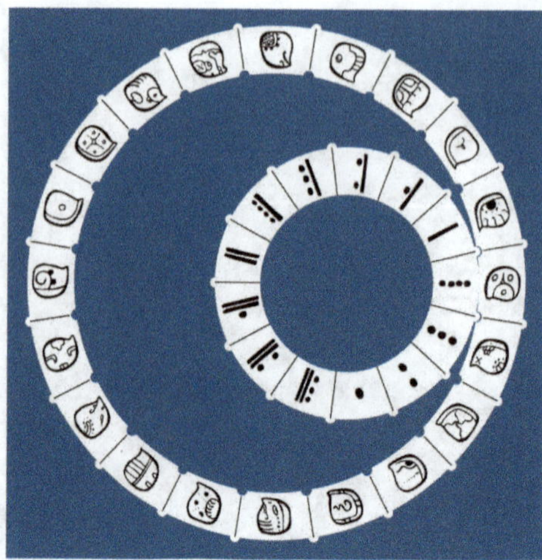

Maya calendar that illustrates the rotation of days

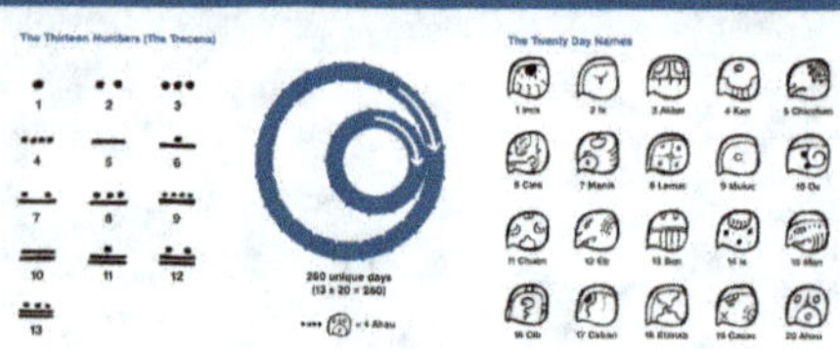

"The days of each of these calendars, changing cyclically according to a specific order, ended up making the two calendars meet again at the same starting point every 52 years, when the cycle began again", explains Paul Gendrop in his work *The Maya civilization.*

The Maya calendars were based on the belief that the world has temporal cycles, and that these, from time to time, repeat themselves. Thanks to this, the two calendars meet again.

"Just as the Sun, Moon, and planets have orbits or cycles that repeat, so did Maya calendars. The Maya believed that history repeated itself and that if a certain date brought misfortune, the next time around it would bring misfortune again. Only by identifying days of bad omens could Maya kings, priests, and shamans perform the proper rituals to ward off the evil", adds Jill Rubalcaba in the work *Empires of the Maya.*

THE LEGEND ABOUT THE BIRTH OF THE MONTHS

The Maya had legends for all types of phenomena, and as if the many that describe gods, men, planets and the creation of everything in the world were not enough, they also had legends focused on the creation of time, and consequently, of its measurements - such as months, days and years. Described in the Chilam Balam book of the month - and later taken up by A. S. Franchini in his work *The best stories from Aztec, Maya and Inca mythologies* - are poetic descriptions of how the days were created, albeit in a somewhat confusing way.

In antiquity, when the world was so young that not even men inhabited its lands, it was impossible to conceive of the counting of its time, not even to obtain the chronological location of its birth. It was then that the month was born, and alone, began its long journey across the planet. Its two grandmothers, its aunt and its sister-in-law had also been walking alone through the world when, heading east, they saw someone's footprints. While they were all distracted by the footprints, the month went further and further, until it decided to create the day, perhaps as a son it was proud of, perhaps as a tiny fraction of its being.

Seeing its beautiful creation, it decided to also create the sky and the Earth, which at first received the strength of a ladder full of rocks, with trees and lots of water. Just like the first day, many others were created, which were called One Chuen, Two Eb, Three Ben and Four Ix, which means "Four Jaguar", in which the Earth and the sky embraced each other. After the Five Men were created, the Earth began to move, until man was created from clay and water in the Thirteen Akbal. The first month was formed when the 20th day was reached.

Experts' interpretation of the topic is very diverse. However, the 20 days of the month have a certain symbolic representation of human life, as shown by A. S. Franchini in his work: "The 20 days were called 'the footprints of the god', and are a symbolic representation of human life and its spiritual journey towards the divine, and it is no coincidence that the first step, or day, was called Imix, a word that comes from Im, or womb. On the second day, called Ik, or 'wind', it is symbolized that the child begins to breathe. In the third, Akbal, they are born through water (the Maya believed in a type of baptism). And so on, until reaching the 20th day, called Ahau, or 'God', where the spiritual journey is completed with the fusion of man with divinity", adds A. S. Franchini.

THE VIEW OF TIME AND THE DUALITY OF LIFE

The notion of time in Mesoamerica, and not only in the Maya interpretation, was seen as an advancement in several cycles governed by the gods, but in addition, it accompanied a consciousness that transcended models of duality. "The Aztec and Maya considered that the universe was structured according to a duality of elements of divine origin (life and death, day and night, light and darkness, wet and dry, the celestial kingdom and the kingdom of hell), which balanced each other and used to follow each other", says Charles Phillips in the work *The Aztec and Maya World*.

The Maya considered the Milky Way, which constantly appeared in the night sky of Mesoamerica, as a large serpent with two heads, one representing death and the other life. Maya diviners could interpret earthly facts and even celestial movements based on temporal conceptions and the vision of duality, allowing it to alter the point of view even on future events. "They accurately measured and dated the movement of the Sun, Moon, and planets. Dates were sculpted on temples, carved on monuments, and painted on pottery. This illustrates the importance of timekeeping to the Maya", adds Jill Rubalcaba in the work *Empires of the maya*.

THE MAYA IN MATHEMATICS

The Maya had one of the most complex numerical systems in all of Mesoamerica, which allowed them to make impressive advances in the assembly of their calendars and events, as well as in the study of astronomy and the counting of goods, among other activities. They were the first to understand the complicated concept of the number zero, and even had a symbol to represent it, many centuries before it was used in Europe. "In addition, the Dresden Codex, which was written during the Postclassic Era, includes multiplication tables—proof that by that time the ancient Maya were performing abstract calculations with their numbers", says Jill Rubalcaba.

In fact, the Maya had the ability to do extremely complicated calculations for a civilization that still used simple and rudimentary tools for its tasks. Today, modern societies use a decimal accounting system, based on the number 10, while the Maya used a vigesimal system, based on the number 20. This system was based, purely and simply, on counting your fingers. "Maya counting system used the human body and all its digits, fingers and toes", states Jill Rubalcaba in her work.

MAYA NUMEROLOGY – THE LONG COUNT

The Maya had another system of counting time to commemorate royal births, accessions to the throne and war victories, among other achievements. Time was counted from a date, a zero point, which in the Gregorian calendar is August 11, 3114 B.C.

Dates were recorded according to five size units: 144 thousand days (Baktun), 7,200 days (Katun), 360 days (tun), 20 days (uinal) and one day (kin). Kings and the elite celebrated the end of a Katun with festivals and monuments that were erected in honor of royalty. "Each Katun was identified with a number and related to a series of prophecies: diviners, rulers and common people hoped that the Katun in question would not differ too much from the previous Katun that bore the same number", explains Charles Phillips in his work *The Aztec and Maya world.*

Certain numbers had sacred meanings for the Maya. The number three was sacred for the three strata: heaven, earth and the underworld. 13 was sacred thanks to the number of celestial planes, while nine was sacred because it was the number of strata of the infraworld.

MAYA COSMOGRAPHY AND ITS WORLDS

The Maya universe would be divided into four levels, with the Cosmic Tree as its main link according to its cosmography, which would be the description of the world and the universe according to the Maya vision. Trees, because they are connected with the three worlds according to the Maya's vision - which would be the heavens, the surface and the underground - have always played a main role in the narratives and were the object of their reverence.

The Ixché Tree, often identified as a Ceiba, but which could also be a paineira, connected these four planes of the world. For the Maya, it was as if the universe had four portions and the cosmic tree was in the center next to the Earth. The Earth is called, in this representation, the middle world, and appears in Maya representations as a turtle, a crocodile or a shark. Inside the quadrangle, on each of the four sides there is a mountain and inside there is a cave with a tree planted.

These four passages give access to a liquid band that is suspended between the Earth and the underworld, inhabited by the dead, supernatural monsters and subterranean gods. The guardian of this ocean is Sak Baak Chapaat, which in the Maya language means "Serpent with White Bones".

Heaven, like the two other worlds, is also divided into four portions, each of which is supported by one of Itzámna's children, the Bakab. "[...] a kind of mythical giant that has the appearance of an old man with the shell of a tortoise or snail (the four Bakabs are respectively called Hobnil, Cantzicnal, Saccimi and Hosanek)", says A. S. Franchini in the work The best stories from Aztec, Maya and Inca mythologies. The Maya sky is also represented by a giant or two-headed crocodile. At the top of the representations of the Maya universe, the god Itzamná is represented as an immense Bird-God.

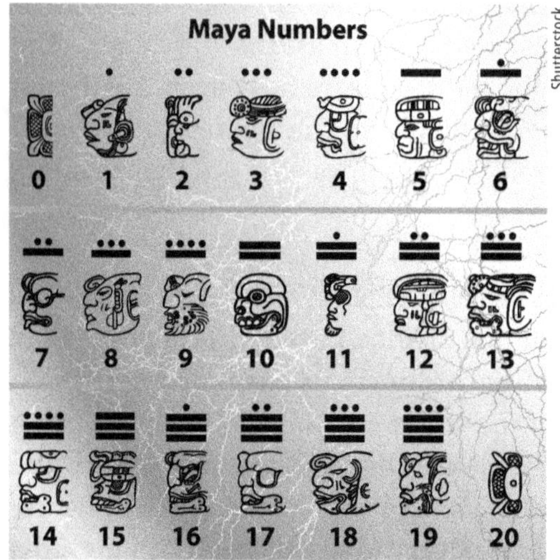

Table with
Maya numbers

12

DISCOVER THE PAINTING, POTTERY, MUSIC AND
ALL THE ARTISTIC PRODUCTION OF THESE PEOPLE

The production system for Maya art pieces, which could also be used as utensils, such as pots or vases, was very cooperative and sometimes resembled the mass production process of many companies. Maya potters, even without using the wheel to speed up the process, are a good example of this mass production. Ceramics were mass-produced on an assembly line and they used molds to make the basic shapes and added decorations by hand. Each step of the manufacturing process was done by a specialist, who passed it on to the next specialist on the assembly line.

This was a technique used by ceramists, but it did not diminish in any way the precision and quality of their work or that of other artists and artisans who worked, among other things, making large mural paintings inside and outside temples, ceramic pieces and sculptures, as well as works in gold and jade. Painters made their brushes with cassava fibers or animal or human hair connected to hollow tubes. Tools were made with sharp points for more detailed work, while the inside of a shell made it the perfect little pot for mixing paints and pigments for work.

Paints were made from different materials, depending on their colors. The yellow, blue and white were made from clay, while the red came from iron oxide. The black was achieved with charcoal, while the brown came from limonite, a mineral.

Maya artisans were also responsible for making the paper that contained the sacred writings and which made it possible to manufacture the various books that still survive in the 21st century. This paper was made from the inner layer of fig tree bark. After soaking in a mixture, it was boiled in water along with corn and lime, or mixed with ash. After receiving this wash, it dried in the sun, until it was dry enough to be smoothed by rubbing with stones or beaten to become finer. To prevent it from breaking, the paper received a thin layer of plaster at the end of the process. "The most talented artisans worked in palace workshops making high-quality goods that brought prestige to their owners. Most, if not all, of those artisans were elite themselves", adds Jill Rubalcaba in the work Empires of the Maya.

MAYA PAINTINGS

Maya paintings have been used, since the beginning of civilization, to create a variety of scenes that go from showing the imagination of their gods and the mythology of that people, to illustrating scenes of wars, battles, glory and governments. Bonampak, one of the Maya cities that was immortalized as an archaeological site and is located next to the Lanchna River, in Mexico, means "Painted Walls", and houses the "Temple of Paintings", one of the most important architectural works in history, for containing the most beautiful painted murals of all the Maya people art. Inside the temple you can see three rooms. The first depicts scenes of preparations for a war expedition while a king is being fawned over by a court and priests. In the second room, the Maya ruler is seen grabbing a prisoner by the hair, while he submits to the king's will, demonstrating a clear sign of humiliation and defeat, illustrating the victory of the Maya in the war.

In the third and final room you can see the frescoes from the party given in honor of the victorious king in his war. According to Charles Phillips, Bonampak's murals represent the apogee of Maya paintings and are characterized by a fluid and expressive style, with an incomparable naturalism.

MAYA MUSIC
The Maya did not have music as developed as their contemporaries, the Aztecs, but they used music in different types

Bonampak's second fresco

of dances and festivities. Maya instruments were very varied and ranged from drums to wind instruments.

Maya drums were the most diverse of all instruments. The Tunkul was a vertical drum made from a hollow tree bark with deer skin at its ends, and often reached up to the percussionist's chest because of its size. The drum made from turtle shells was played with the hands, unlike another type of smaller drum made from wooden membranes, which was necessarily played with drumsticks.

There were also drums made of clay that were in the shape of two jars placed base by base and with membranes at the ends. Dancers, during ritual dances, often tied copper, gold and silver bells to their wrists, legs and waists while playing with their hands a small drum called a pax.

The wind instruments received slightly more sinister materials. Musicians played flutes made from cane, shells, and even human leg bones. There were also clay or wooden trumpets.

"Music was not limited to happy occasions. Drummers marched shoulder to shoulder with warriors into battle. Bands of musicians led funeral processions. special whistles were carved for funerals. the notes were supposed to capture the attention of the gods to let them know a loved one had embarked on their journey through the underworld", adds Jill Rubalcaba in the work *Empires of the Maya*.

13

PYRAMIDS, TEMPLES AND CITIES HIDDEN IN THE
DENSE FORESTS OF MESOAMERICA

Maya architecture is a subject of fascination and arouses our curiosity about this great civilization, largely due to the legacy that remained intact within the Guatemalan jungles for centuries until they were discovered. Pyramids, temples and even entire cities are still discovered to this day, due to their difficult location and because they are hidden in the densest Mesoamerican vegetation.

However, it is impressive how the Maya left such a legacy using only rudimentary construction techniques, as Jill Rubalcaba explains in her work *Empires of the Maya:* "The Maya built these great cities using Stone Age technology. They had no cement to make walls or steel to provide reinforcement or bear loads. There were no metal tools—no metal saws, drills, or carving tools. All their tools were made of stone."

MAYA CONSTRUCTION TECHNIQUES

Maya construction techniques, since the earliest times of this civilization, followed a logical pattern for the construction of a building, whether public, private or even temples and pyramids. First, the Maya erected four resistant pillars made of adobe paste and intertwined several thin sticks inside them, to provide greater support. These four pillars were placed in this way in honor of the legend of the sons of the god Itzamná, who placed his four sons one in each corner of the earth, in order to hold up the heavens. Once this was done, the Maya builders moved on to building the walls, which could be made of stones in larger buildings or in places that had an abundance of stones. "In some regions, where there was stone to build on, builders placed stone platforms for houses or built the lower parts of walls in stone before covering them with adobe or lime paste", says Charles Phillips in the work *The Aztec and Maya World.*

Many of the buildings built in the hottest regions of Central America were built by the Maya without covering the walls, to allow greater air circulation, as the houses did not have windows. Once the walls were finished, the Maya built the roofs at an angle in which the flat sheets they used, or even straw, would not be so damaged by heavy rains, making the buildings true shelters for the Maya people. "The stone temples were more elaborate and permanent versions of the ancestral hut. The elements of the primitive house were

Ruins of the city of Uxmal, in Mexico

reproduced in the palace and the temple", says Charles Phillips in his work.

SOUND AND LIGHT EFFECTS

Maya architecture has always had great proportions and the temples and pyramids left by this great civilization are still studied today. A curious fact that scholars have been able to confirm is that some of its temples may have been designed according to the effects of light and sound. Acoustics was very important for the Maya, because thanks to it a priest could declaim ritual speeches so that everyone could hear. "Recent work by scholars has suggested that ritual complexes and sacred squares may have been designed with acoustics in mind," says Charles Phillips in the work *The Aztec and Maya World*.

In fact, the first to recognize that the Maya had an architectural project that was much more complex than it seemed was the acoustic engineer and consultant at the University of Southern California, David Lubman. In 1998, on his expedition to the Maya lands, Lubman noticed how the steps of the pyramid returned the sound that was made when clapping at the base of the stairs. The sound that returned was similar to the descending cry of a quetzal bird, considered a sacred animal to the Maya. Lubman further argues in his thesis that the steps were carefully positioned so that this bird cry sound was possible. To achieve this, the Maya combined a narrow base on the lower steps (where the foot rests) with a higher counter base (height of the step).

Another effect studied was that of lights. It was discovered that the Temple of the Feathered Serpent was built in that location because it was where the spring and autumn equinoxes formed a pattern of undulating light on the steps of the pyramid, like a kind of serpent of light.

CHICHÉN ITZA

Chichén Itzá, which literally means "Itzá at the edge of the well" in Mayan dialects, is located at the tip of the Yucatán Peninsula, on one of the strips of land that advances towards the ocean.

RAW MATERIALS FOR CONSTRUCTION

The raw materials used in large Maya constructions varied according to availability and region. In the southern region, rocks that were easy to model were not easily found, forcing the Maya to use other resources. "Even the largest buildings were often made of adobe blocks, although in Copán the workers extracted and used local trachyte and in Kiriguá they worked with marble, sandstone and rhyolite", says Charles Phillips in his work.

In the northernmost regions, large quantities of limestone could be found easily, and because it was a rich material and easy to cut into blocks, workers were able to work much better. Furthermore, it was possible to make plaster by burning lime.

Perhaps the most famous Maya city of all, Chichén Itzá apparently - according to Maya accounts described in Chilam Balam - was founded by the god Itzamná himself after a long pilgrimage by the Maya people.

More important than the founding of the city under the wings of the god, was the revolutionary political system that Chichén Itzá brought to the legacy of the Maya. The Itzá practiced a decentralized form of government, which was a rarity for the time. Power was in the hands of a king, but also of a governing council, formed by the leaders of noble families and the elite. This system was called Multepal (mul means "group" and tepal means "to rule"). "Each person held a particular administrative position in a specific territory. Now issues were discussed among many people before arriving at a joint decision", tells Jill Rubalcaba in the work Empires of the Maya. The security of this new political regime was a great achievement for the Maya, because, if the king of the city was captured during an invasion or military incursion, the city would not be left unprotected and without command.

Temple of Kukulcán in Chichén Itzá, Mexico, is one of the seven wonders of the modern world

Chichén Itzá was also a cultural landmark for the Maya. With a much more outward-looking thinking, the nobles added their influence within the city itself and its public spaces. "In addition, the leaders of the city promoted the exchange of goods and ideas throughout Mesoamerica. By adopting customs from outsiders, expanding trade networks, and welcoming immigrants, Chichén Itzá enlarged its cultural tradition", adds Jill Rubalcaba in her work.

THE DECLINE

It is still unclear to historians why Chichén Itzá was abandoned and consequently destroyed. Its construction stopped in A.D 1050, and by A.D 1100 the city was no longer the dominant center of the Yucatán peninsula. In 1300, it was completely replaced by the sister city of Mayapán in command of the regional league, a pact that united a triple alliance between Chichén Itzá, Mayapán and Uxmal. "Historians are unsure if Chichén Itzá's ruin came about through conquest by other peoples or if the destruction occurred after the downfall", adds Jill Rubalcaba.

PALENQUE

Palenque is, like Chichén Itzá, one of the most famous Maya cities. Located on the northern edge of what is now the Mexican state of Chiapas, the city also houses one of the most important archaeological sites for understanding the Maya people.

Considered by historian Jacques Soustelle as "The City of Refinement and Grace", Palenque was in essence different from other Maya city-states of the classical period. There were no sumptuous groves of stelae in which Maya carvers put the art of hieroglyphic writing into practice, nor vast ceremonial squares, acropolises or great commercial roads. The main difference was in other details, mentioned by Charles Phillips in the work *The Aztec and Maya World:* "His buildings were adorned with stucco sculptures and reliefs, pioneers in the art of naturalistic portraiture of royal figures".

Still, the city was one of the largest in the Maya world and achieved a prestigious position in Mesoamerican politics during the years A.D 615 to 683, a time when King Pakal assumed the throne of Palenque and became the largest ruler of the entire history of the city.

KING PAKAL

Hanab Pakal was one of the most brilliant Maya rulers who ever lived. His reign lasted approximately 67 years and brought much prosperity to the city of Palenque and himself, with the creation of monuments that illustrated the honor of the gods and the myths of creation. "When Hanab Pakal took the throne at 12 years old, he marked the beginning of a new dynasty in Palenque", says Jill Rubalcaba when highlighting the importance of the king's legacy in the work Empires of the Maya. Gaining everyone's support, King Pakal set in motion a major construction program that built, among others, the monuments known today as the Forgotten Temple and the Palace Complex.

King Pakal's body still rests under a five-ton lid in the great Temple of the Inscriptions, discovered in 1952 by Mexican archaeologist Alberto Ruz. After his death, his son Chan-Bahlum assumed the throne.

THE DECLINE

Palenque's decline was far from glorious or epic. Chan-Bahlum's brother, Kan Xul, assumed the throne after Bahlum's 18-year reign. However, it only caused problems for everyone. Eager for conquests, he organized an incursion to capture the leader of one of the neighboring tribes, but he was the one who ended up captured. However, according to Maya laws, they could not replace Kan Xul with another king until he was sacrificed. As a military strategy, the rival tribe left him alive for many years, causing Palenque to gradually collapse due to the absence of its leader. When Kan Xul was sacrificed, Palenque was just a shadow of what it once was, and even with a sequence of rulers, it disappeared gradually and silently.

TIKAL

Tikal means "the place of voices" in the Mayan language, and for more than a thousand years the Maya continued to build in the city, making it one of the oldest Maya cities of all time.

The city began its expansion when it was still just a simple village, in the pre-classic phase of the Maya period, and over time it grew until it became the great power it came to be. "Located in Guatemala, the city, considered the largest of all in the Maya world, is full of stelae that provide us with its precise chronological history, giving us an indication, step by step, of its beginning (A.D 292), going through its heyday, until its decline, around A.D 869.", says A. S. Franchini in his work.

At its peak, the city had more than 60 thousand inhabitants. For a long time, as occurred in several Mesoamerican cities at that time, the people around Tikal suffered pauses in the production of their monuments. This could have occurred through an alliance with a neighboring kingdom or through the fall of the rulers, the latter being what actually happened countless times within the political history of the people around the city, as well as the Maya of Tikal.

THE SPLENDOR

After the fall of El Mirador, one of the youngest Maya centers during the Preclassic era, many communities, which were previously small, had the opportunity to base their policies and expand their domains over Mesoamerica. One of these communities was Tikal, which long emerged as a true power. George Stuart and Gene Stuart describe a little about the size the

Pyramid of the Lost World, located in the oldest part of Tikal

city had at its peak, in the work *Lost Kingdoms of the Maya*. According to the authors, Tikal had more than six square miles in its central area alone, which could fit more than 3 thousand buildings with roads connecting them all, where temples, pyramids, palaces, ball fields, squares and houses predominated.

Thanks to this immense complex rich in constructions, archeology has taken a great step toward an almost inexhaustible source of knowledge about the Maya. More than 100,000 objects have been discovered from the ruins of Tikal, and it is impossible to calculate how many still exist in its soil. "The ancient residential zone sprawls over more than 23 square miles of forest", George and Gene say in their work.

THE DECLINE

After a series of years-long conflicts involving Calakmul, another local tribe that defeated the inhabitants of Tikal, in 869 the 33rd king and last ruler of Tikal failed to rebuild the conflict-ravaged city. Even so, for unknown reasons, the inhabitants of Tikal separated into small communities, while the glorious city was lost in the middle of the dense jungles, being swallowed by nature until its rediscovery by archaeologists.

COPÁN

Copán was one of the largest Maya cities of the classic period and remains one of the most important archaeological sites for understanding the civilization, with several iconic buildings. Located west of Honduras, on the dividing line that separates that country from Guatemala, the city is at an altitude of 700 meters in the Copán River Valley, and for centuries was occupied by several peoples, since 1000 B.C. "Copán dominated the southeastern Maya area through a long, unbroken line of 16 rulers. [...] Copán's rich resources supported its growth during this period of stability. The polity was located on fertile agricultural lands. It was also strategically positioned on important trade routes", says Jill Rubalcaba in the work *Empires of the Maya*.

Its rich lands caused the city's population to grow exponentially in a short period of time, which caused Copán to grow outside of the Valley's dependencies. At its peak, which was around A.D

800, Copán had more than 20 thousand inhabitants, including the villages that were located in the city's immediate vicinity.

THE CONSTRUCTIONS

The constructions found in Copán significantly illustrate the splendor of the Maya civilization thanks to a set of stelae, which are large stones carved with different hieroglyphs, which tell the story of the people.

Another very important construction, and perhaps the most notable in the entire city, is the Hieroglyphic Stairway which, located on the west face of a pyramid in the city center, is one of the most complete records of the history of the Maya people. "Full of terraces and platforms, the 'Athens of the Maya' presents its relics, such as the Hieroglyphic Stairway, formed by 63 steps adorned by 2,500 glyphs – the longest inscription found in Maya monuments -, in which the names of the reigning sovereigns and a series of historical events that have not yet been completely deciphered are inscribed [...]", says A. S. Franchini in the work *As Melhores Histórias das Mitologias Asteca, Maia e Inca*.

The city also had ball courts of imposing dimensions, as well as an Acropolis, which in addition to being the largest building in the entire city, also included two large courtyards and several temples.

The Acropolis was on the south side of the city, while on the north side remained the ball courts, the staircase and the Great Square. From this Great Square there were several roads heading towards the cities and towns further north, as well as the region containing the residences.

THE DECLINE

After the death of Lord Smoke-Jaguar in 695, and the capture of Lord XVIII-jog some time later, the fate of Copán was in the hands of King Smoke-Shell, the 15th ruler. He was responsible for the construction of the Hieroglyphic Stairway, as well as the formation of a council made up of elites to assist the king. To give more strength and autonomy to Copán, which had already lost a large part of its commercial routes, King Smoke-Shell married one of the daughters of Palenque's royalty.

In 810, his son Yax Pac had just assumed the throne when nobles and local city leaders seized the remainder of Copán's territories and expelled the royalty from their rightful place, thus ending the dynasty of rulers as well as the glory of Copán.

Ancient engraving from Copán, 1890

14

THE ARRIVAL OF THE SPANIARDS

WITH THE INVASION OF THE EUROPEANS, THE MAYA CIVILIZATION WAS HARDLY ATTACKED, WENT INTO DECLINE AND ITS CITIES WERE ABANDONED

The arrival of the Spaniards in the lands of Central America was not at all glorious. The first contact with the Maya only occurred during Christopher Columbus' last trip to the Americas, in 1502. However, the first Spanish attack on the Maya was not with their muskets, but with diseases. "By 1516, the Maya of the Yucatán had been devastated by what was probably smallpox. The Maya had never been exposed to smallpox before the arrival of the Spaniards, and they had no immunity", says Jill Rubalcaba in the work *Empires of the Maya.*

The first frontal attack by the Spaniards on the Maya occurred in 1519, led by Hernán Cortés, who also conquered the Aztecs. However, even with the advantage of having more sophisticated equipment and horses, it took the Spaniards approximately 200 years to subject the Maya to their will. By the time the Spaniards ended their offensive, the Maya population had been reduced by 90%.

THE ABANDONMENT OF CITIES AND THE END OF CIVILIZATION

As ironic as this may be, the Maya themselves brought about their defeat. When the Spaniards arrived, they still possessed, in almost their entire territory, the political bases that divided them into several city-states. As if the entire civilization was not divided enough, many of these cities were weakened due to internal tribal attacks. Thanks to new diseases, the Spaniards had a slightly more open path to conquest. However, the main factor was the attitude of the Maya themselves. To destroy rival cities, they allied with the Spaniards to massacre the Maya in other locations. After achieving victory, the Spaniards turned against their former allies, promoting their equal downfall.

THE MAYA AND THEIR ARRIVAL IN THE 20TH CENTURY

After the European conquest and colonization, another historical episode was decisive in the lives of the Maya. The regions of Central America were already in the process of becoming the nations we know today, and the Maya, in the midst of this political context, had to adapt to survive the changing times.

THE HACIENDAS

When the Mexicans rebelled against the Spaniards in 1810,

and after a long war that lasted until 1821, they did indeed achieve independence, and the Maya living on the Yucatán peninsula were as relieved as the Mexicans at the end of Spanish oppression. Little did they know that their position within society had not actually gained any advancement. "Although the Maya were now technically a free people within a new nation, the majority had no way to support themselves other than working on the farms owned by wealthy landowners" explains Jill Rubalcaba in the work *Empires of the Maya*. These farms were all run by descendants of the original Spanish conquistadors. The life of the Maya in these haciendas (Spanish term for farms) was no better than that of slaves. "The Spanish landowners took advantage of the Maya's situation and controlled them by keeping the Maya in financial debt. They were never paid enough wages to work off their debt, and so they were forced to keep working on the haciendas. [...] They lived in extreme poverty", says Jill Rubalcaba in her work.

The Mexican government, which was dealing with a series of revolts among its own population, realized the situation that the Maya were going through and offered them the opportunity to serve the Mexican army in exchange for forgiveness of their debts with the *haciendas*. In 1847, however, the Maya organized an armed rebellion against the descendants of the original Spaniards and the Mexicans, realizing that they would never escape that situation.

ATHE WAR OF THE CASTES

On July 30, 1847, after more than three centuries of abuse at the hands of Europeans and their descendants, the Maya began their violent armed revolt in search of freedom. With a force of 12 to 15 thousand soldiers, they expelled several Spaniards from their lands and set them on fire. "Maya soldiers in the Yucatán massacred men, women, and children. [...] In an effort to put down the rebellion, Mexican authorities drafted all men from age 16 to 60 into the army. Both sides committed cruel and brutal acts", says Jill Rubalcaba in her work.

As early as 1850, the Maya had settled in an independent community of the *haciendas*, in the village of Chan Santa Cruz. There, they set up a camp that resisted Mexican military forces for more than 50 years.

The turnaround would occur in the 20th century, when, in an agreement with Mexico, the United Kingdom, which provided supplies and weapons for the Maya, refused to continue supplying them, causing the Maya to lose their battle against the Mexicans in 1901. "The War of the Castes had cost the Maya dearly. More than 50,000 Maya lost their lives in the rebellion", adds Jill Rubalcaba in the work *Empires of the Maya.*

MEXICO AND THE MAYA

In 1915, the Mexican government removed all military forces from Chan Santa Cruz and from those lands the Maya regained control of their own paths. Small villages were formed on the outskirts of that region and another type of religious belief, a mixture of Spanish Christianity and Maya polytheism was created and followed by these people.

The Maya of Yucatán got good jobs at that time thanks to an economic *boom* of Henequen – a type of fibrous plant that was used to make yarn – which was in great demand in countries such as the United States. However, prices for this material fell drastically with the collapse of the New York Stock Exchange in 1929, and as a result, the Yucatán region went from the most promising to the poorest in just a few decades. "Maya workers could not find jobs. Crime rose as quickly as the poverty levels. Today, the people of Yucatán look to tourism as a way of building jobs and opportunities", adds Jill Rubalcaba in the work *Empires of the Maya.*

15

GUATEMALA: THE HEART OF THE MAYA

WHAT IS LEFT OF THESE PEOPLE IN CENTRAL AMERICAN COUNTRIES AND HOW PART OF THE TRADITIONS ARE PRESERVED TODAY

Maya buildings, cities and territories are located in different parts of Central America and today occupy around five countries, which use Maya culture and its remains to promote their tourism: Mexico, El Salvador, Guatemala, Honduras and Belize.

The campaigns involving the ancient culture of the Amerindian people revolve around the prophecies that constituted the end of the world, according to scholars.

The Maya people are actually the union of several peoples, a characteristic that makes them similar to the ancient Greeks, who never constituted a unified State. Another aspect that makes the Maya resemble the ancient Greeks is their great artistic and scientific development.

Maya culture is alive and ancient traditions are maintained in these countries.

Architecture is represented in temples, palaces and pyramids with steps.

Spanish Baroque is present in colonial architecture, represented by indigenous elements. An example of this style is present in the ruins of the San Jose cathedral, located in the city of Antigua Guatemala. Its construction began in 1542, with

Tourist visiting ancient Maya ruins in Guatemala

the pillars placed next to the old cathedral in the Almolonga Valley, and was interrupted due to frequent earthquakes in the region. In 1669 the temple was demolished and a new sanctuary was inaugurated in 1680, under the direction of Juan Pascual and José de Porres. The title of cathedral was granted in 1743, making it the most luxurious in Central America at the time. Under its structure there is a crypt and a set of tunnels of unknown value.

Maya sculptural art, made of plaster, stone and wood, was decorative and decorated temples and palaces. In 2019, Polish archaeologists found more than 800 Maya objects while diving in Lake Peten Itza, in northern Guatemala. Among the objects were ceremonial cups and obsidian rock blades, from the period A.D 1000 to A.D 1697, possibly used for animal sacrifices. Maya's popular statuary reached perfection from the 16th century onwards.

In Guatemala there are some of the most remote remains of the Maya civilization, whose phases are known thanks to stone stelae, used to measure time. The first stele dates back to A.D 328, found in Uaxactún. Stelas telling the deeds of a certain king were part of the landscape of Maya public squares. Other centers with Maya ruins are Quirigua and Yaxchilán.

GUATEMALA: THE HEART OF THE MAYAN WORLD

Half of the more than 20 million people in Guatemala are Maya. However, unlike Mexico, even though they make up almost half of the active population, in Guatemala they still suffer prejudice, being considered inferior in relation to their Spanish descendants.

The history of the Maya in Guatemala was as difficult as in Mexican lands. Maya farmers, still in the middle of the 20th century, were expelled from their lands to mountainous areas where agriculture was terribly difficult and very unproductive.

At the time, the Guatemalan government, between 1945 and 1954, tried in every way to treat the Maya with more dignity, despite the government of the United States of America intervening heavily on behalf of the coalition of North American companies *American United Fruit Company* (AUFC), which owned more land in Guatemala than any other company.

Thus, to prevent the fall in profits, the North American government helped in the overthrow of the Guatemalan government, which lost its position to a military dictatorship in 1954.

"The new military government was so corrupt that thousands of Maya chose to flee their homeland in fear for their lives. Those who remained and spoke out against the corruption were imprisoned or executed", says Jill Rubalcaba in the work *Empires of the Maya.*

Even with the flight of thousands of Maya, more than 150 thousand people were killed and another 40 thousand remained missing. In the 1980s alone, thousands fled to camps in Mexico or the United States.

The Maya suffering in Guatemala would only end in 1995, with the election of the conservative Alvaro Arzú, who governed from 1996 to 2000. Today, things are far from being similar to what happened during the military government. The Maya can celebrate their cultural identity and have returned to their ancestral lands, all under the protection of the law.

Multiculturalism and historical roots are the main strategies for promoting tourism in Guatemala, which have been explored since the 1990s.

THE MAYA TODAY

It is estimated that there are today around 6 million Maya descendants. The second main indigenous ethnic group in Mexico, after the Nahuas, the Maya represent 80% of the population of Yucatán, a state in the south of the country. In addition, there are also communities in Belize, Guatemala, Honduras and El Salvador.

They constitute some isolated tribes in the territories of the different countries in which they were a dominant presence centuries ago, with the exception of Guatemala, which still has a large proportion of Maya in its population.

However, the tendency is for Maya customs to dissipate over the years, as happened with the group of Maya who live in the Mexican state of Chiapas.

The Lacandon, as they are called, are a Maya tribe that still speaks one of the 30 Mayan dialects and continues to preserve the same customs as their ancestors. They live in houses with thatched roofs and the women still produce fabrics using techniques from that period, and on them, they embroider images of their ancestors, their gods and creeds, while the men still go to the corn fields and get together to build houses.

However, one of the last Maya chiefs, Chan K'in, who still played his role as a priest and offered clay pots to the gods, died in 1996. Today, the pots are sold by his son to tourists in Palenque. From there, one by one, the younger Maya slowly abandon their roots to join the contemporary world.

Man with traditional clothes in Guatemala

BIBLIOGRAPHIC REFERENCES

DEVINE, Jennifer. The maya spirit: tourism and multiculturalism in post peace accords Guatemala. **London Journal of Tourism, Sport and Creative Industries (LJTSCI)**, Volume 2, Edition 1, Spring 2009. Disponível em https://www.jenniferdevine.com/uploads/3/7/8/2/37825821/devine_the_maya_spirit.pdf acesso em 3/8/2022.

ESTRADA-BELLI, Francisco. **The first maya civilization**. Boston: Ed. Routledge, 2010.

FRANCHINI, A. S. **As melhores histórias das mitologias asteca, maia e inca.** São Paulo: Ed. Artes e Ofícios, 2012.

GENDROP, Paul. **A civilização maia**. São Paulo: Zahar Editora, 1987.

LANDA, Diego de. **Relación de las cosas de Yucatán**. Madrid: Alianza Editorial, 2017.

LANDA. Diego de. **Yucatán before and after the conquest**. Nova York: Dover Publications, 2012.

PHILLIPS, Charles. **O mundo asteca e maia**. São Paulo: Editora Folio, 2002.

RUBALCABA, Jill. **Empires of the maya**. Nova York: Chelsea House Publishers, 2009.

SHARER, Robert J. **The ancient maya**. Redwood City: Stanford University Press, 2005.

SMITH, Monica L. **The social construction of ancient cities**. Smithsonian Books, 2010.

SOMERVILL, Barbara A. **Empire of the aztecs**. The Commercial Press, 2015.

STUART, George e STUART, Gene. **Lost kingdoms of the maya**. National Geographic Society, 1993.

WILLIAMS, Carlos Rivera. Historia de la medicina y cirugía en América: la civilización maya. **Revista Médica Hondureña** (2007; 75:152-158).

CHECK OUT OUR NEW
RELEASES HERE!

Camelot
EDITORA